D1276418

coffee
cup
Bible
studies

Premium Roast with
Ruth

Advancing the Ministries of the Gospel

AMG Publishers

God's Word to you is our highest calling.

SANDRA GLAHN

Coffee Cup Bible Studies
Premium Roast with Ruth

© 2007 by Sandra L. Glahn

Published by AMG Publishers. All Rights Reserved.

Published in association with the literary
agency of Alive Communications, Inc., 7860 Goddard Street, Suite 200,
Colorado Springs, Colorado, 80920

First Printing, 2007

ISBN 10: 0-89957-236-9
ISBN 13: 978-089957236-7

Unless otherwise noted, Scripture is taken from the NET Bible.
Copyright © 1996–2005 by Biblical Studies Press (www.bible.org). Used by
permission.

Scripture quotations marked (NASB) are from the New American Standard
Bible®. Copyright © 1960, 1962, 1963, 1968, 1971, 1972, 1973, 1975,
1977, 1995, by The Lockman Foundation. Used by permission.
(www.Lockman.org)

Scripture quotations marked (NIV) are from the Holy Bible, New
International Version, copyright 1973, 1978, 1984, International Bible
Society. Used by permission of Zondervan Publishing House

Editing and Proofreading: Candy Arrington and Rick Steele
Interior Design: PerfecType, Nashville, Tennessee
Cover Design: ImageWright Marketing and Design, Chattanooga, Tennessee

Printed in the United States of America
11 10 09 08 07 06 –D– 6 5 4 3 2 1

ACKNOWLEDGMENTS

- Gary—My beloved husband and ministry partner, you embody *hesed*. Thank you for your loyal love and for totally believing in me long before I believed in myself.

- Drs. Bob Chisholm and Jeffrey Watson—You labored to teach me Hebrew. Thank you for making a rigorous task enjoyable, even sometimes fun.

- Members of Biblical Studies Press (bible.org) and translators of the NET Bible—Without you and the help of your vital ministry, the Coffee Cup Bible Study series would not even be possible. Thank you for laboring without compensation so others might grow in the Word.

- Chip MacGregor—Thanks for representing me enthusiastically, for finding a home for this series, and for your boundless encouragement.

- Alison Mullins—I so appreciate your hospitality, your editorial suggestions, and your great observations on the Book of Ruth. Thank you for generously sharing your notes and your self.

- Virginia Swint—One such friend in a lifetime is more than most people even hope for. Thank you for your endless support, your example of quiet service, and your careful eye for detail.

- Jacob Glidewell—Thanks for reading carefully, offering some of your favorite verbs, and for taking time to express how this story affected you.

- Dan Penwell of AMG—Thank for your generous encouragement, your testimony of trust, and for championing this series.

- Rick Steele of AMG—Your editing scalpel has saved me from my own typographical, language, and grammatical blunders time and again. Thanks for making me look good.

- Pastor Lance Ward—Your heart for the vulnerable and your faithful exposition of God's Word, particularly this book of the Bible, have blessed, encouraged, and challenged me. I appreciate you, brother.

- Finally to all who are praying that God will use the Word through this series to change lives—May you be abundantly rewarded in public for works done in secret.

INTRODUCTION TO THE
COFFEE CUP BIBLE STUDIES

The precepts of the LORD are right, rejoicing the heart;
The commandment of the LORD is pure, enlightening the eyes
(Psalm 19:8).

Congratulations! You have chosen wisely. In deciding to study the Bible, you are electing to spend time learning that which will rejoice the heart and enlighten the eyes.

And while any study in the Bible is time well spent, the Coffee Cup Bible series has some unique elements that set it apart from others. So before we get started, let's talk about some of those elements designed to help you maximize your study time.

Life Rhythms—Most participants in any Bible study have little problem keeping up during the weekdays, when they have a routine. Yet on the weekends there's a general "falling off." Thus, the *Coffee Cup Bible Studies* contain Monday-through-Friday Bible study questions, but the Saturday and Sunday segments consist of short, more passive readings that draw application and insight from the texts you'll be considering. Know that the days listed here are mere suggestions. Some find it preferable to attend a Bible study one day and follow a four-day-per-week study schedule along with weekend readings. Feel free to change the structure of days and assignments to best fit your own needs.

Community—While the studies in the Coffee Cup series can be completed individually, they are also ideal for group interaction. If you don't have a local group with which to meet, find a few friends and start one. Or connect with others through www.soulpersuit.com, where you can participate, if you like, by engaging in artistic expressions as you interact with the text. These vehicles give you opportunities to share what you're learning with a wider community.

Aesthetics—At the author's Web site (www.aspire2.com) in a section designed for the Coffee Cup series, you will find links to art that depicts what's being discussed, such as "Naomi and Her Daughter-in-law" by Gustave Doré and Rembrandt's "Boaz and Ruth." You'll find motion picture listings, and novels, such as *Ebony Moon*, a retelling of Ruth's story in a modern setting. And you'll also find some musical versions. Engage as many of your five senses as possible in your interaction with God's truth. You might even find recipes that use barley!

Convenience—Rather than looking up references in the Bible, you'll find the entire text for each day included in the Coffee Cup study book (thanks to the Biblical Studies Foundation). While it's important to know our way around the Bible, the Coffee Cup series is designed so you can take it with you and study the Bible on the subway, at a coffee shop, in a doctors' waiting room, or on your lunch break. The chosen translation is the NET Bible, which is accessible via internet from virtually anywhere in the world. You can find more about it, along with numerous textual notes, at www.bible.org, which serves more than 3.5 million people worldwide.

The NET Bible is a modern translation from the ancient Greek, Hebrew, and Aramaic texts. Both the online and text versions of this Bible include 60,932 translators' notes and citations pulling from more than 700 scholarly works.

Sensitivity to time-and-culture considerations—Many Bible studies skip what we call the "theological" step. That is, they go straight from observing and interpreting the words given to those in a different time and culture to applying in a modern-day setting. The result is sometimes misapplication (example—"Paul told slaves to obey their *masters* so we need to obey our *employers*"). In the Coffee Cup series, our aim is to be particularly sensitive to the audience to whom the "mail" was addressed and work to take the crucial step of separating what was intended for a limited audience from that which is for all audiences for all time (love God; love your neighbor).

Sensitivity to genres—Rather than crafting a series in which we approach each book exactly like all the others, each Coffee Cup Bible

Series study is structured to best present the genre being examined—whether epistle, poetry, gospel, history, or narrative. The way we study Ruth, a narrative, differs from how someone might study the dense poetry in Song of Songs. So while the studies in the Coffee Cup series may have similar elements, no two will be quite the same.

INTRODUCTION TO THE BOOK OF RUTH

Tamar seduced her father-in-law. Jael drove a tent peg through a general's head. Rachel stole her father's idols. Rahab engaged in the world's oldest profession. Esther resided as queen over an empire that covered more than ten modern-day countries. And Sarah conceived a baby at ninety.

Do all these exciting women sound like the kind of people you drink coffee with? Me either. So what in the world do twenty-first century women with cell phones and washing machines and SUVs (or earth-friendly hybrids) have in common with them? Our own children, if we have any, may say, "That was back in the day. . . ," when people used phones with cords and record players that turned. Yet we're supposed to identify with women who lived *thousands* of years ago? While their God-sized tasks had national ramifications, God-sized tasks for us look more like keeping the shopping done, mounds of clothes laundered, bills paid, prescriptions filled, dishes washed, and whining quelled. Or maybe our challenges involve dealing with dirty diapers, or nagging bosses, or loveless marriages.

We have much more in common with these women of the past than we might think. Why? Because each of them was, as my friend Mary likes to say, an ordinary woman with an extraordinary God.

Especially Ruth.

Ruth's was an international marriage, until, after a decade of infertility, her sickly husband died young, as did his father and brother.

Ruth endured plenty of loss and poverty. She couldn't spruce up her resume, throw on a pair of heels and go out job seeking, or file for unemployment. She had no education, no training, no pedigree, and no social connections.

Okay, she did have one thing—a sad, widowed mother-in-law who seemed not to appreciate her.

Yet despite her difficulties, Ruth didn't feel sorry for herself. Instead, she trusted in God, sacrificed her own needs for the sake of someone else, and loved the unlovely. As a result, God honored her. Greatly. This little no-name woman of faith went on to become the ancestress to the King of kings and Lord of lords. But I'm getting ahead of myself.

If you're a regular student of Bible study, you know that the inductive Bible Study method is a good and popular approach to studying God's word. It emphasizes considering a biblical text first by observing what it says, then interpreting what it means, and finally by making application to everyday life. This is a particularly fine approach to studying New Testament epistles.

Yet our method must change a bit when we approach Ruth and other stories. When we come to the narratives in scripture, we must consider larger blocks of text at one time to find the application the author intended. If we took the same approach with Ruth that we do with the epistles, we might mistakenly try to draw application from the first few verses in chapter one, when the entire message doesn't appear until we look at the entire story from the perspective of all eighty-five verses. Thus, when studying narratives we need to see the whole story put together before we can see the main point or points the author is making. The inductive approach (observation, interpretation, application) is good in both cases, yet what changes is the size of the sections we consider at one time.

Think about what would happen if we drew conclusions about Aesop's "Boy Who Cried Wolf" story before reading the entire thing:

A shepherd-boy, who watched a flock of sheep near a village, brought out the villagers three or four times by crying out, "Wolf! Wolf!"and when his neighbors came to help him, laughed at them for their pains.

The wolf, however, did truly come at last. The shepherd-boy, now really alarmed, shouted in an agony of terror: "Pray,

2 *Unger's Bible Dictionary*, 831.

do come and help me; the Wolf is killing the sheep"; but no one paid any heed to his cries, nor rendered any assistance. The Wolf, having no cause of fear, at his leisure lacerated or destroyed the whole flock.

There is no believing a liar, even when he speaks the truth.

Now, let's say we read only the first paragraph of Aesop's tale and then tried to "apply this story to our lives." If we didn't read the entire story first, we might come up with some odd "applications":

If you want to really amuse yourself, make up a big, scary story and watch what happens when people believe you.

If you want to get people to act, yell something that will make them sure to act quickly—like "Fire!" in a theatre.

Chances are slim that the so-called application would remotely resemble the one Aesop actually intended.

An inappropriate way to approach Ruth, then, is to zero in on specific parts of the story without first getting the whole idea. We might read Boaz's question to his servant, "To whom does this woman belong" and conclude God says women are merely property. To avoid that sort of gross error, we must pay attention to details within the big picture of the narrative and an understanding of the culture in which the story occurred.

So what are the main points of Ruth's story? We don't see them spelled out like Aesop did with his fable when he concluded, "There is no believing a liar, even when he speaks the truth." Yet after we read the whole amazing drama of Ruth's experience, the picture becomes clear. God restored Ruth, but that restoration extended beyond her lifetime. During a dark time in the nation's history, God continued through Ruth the line that would lead to the great king David and ultimately to Jesus Christ. That tells us that the Almighty...

- Is sovereign over all
- Keeps every promise
- Can reverse impossible situations
- Can bless the faithful, average, normal unextraordinary person more richly and for longer than she could ever imagine.

All that is still true today: Your life matters. God cares for you. The Lord is in control. The Sovereign One is worthy of all trust.

CONTENTS

WEEK 1 OF 4

The Big Picture: Ruth 1–4

Ruth 1:3–5 "Sometime later Naomi's husband Elimelech died, so she and her two sons were left alone. So her sons married Moabite women. (One was named Orpah and the other Ruth.) And they continued to live there about ten years. Then Naomi's two sons, Mahlon and Kilion, also died. So the woman was left all alone—bereaved of her two children as well as her husband!"

A friend asked, "*If you could write a novel on any subject, what would it be?*"

I told her I would love, someday, to know enough about the ancient Near East to write a fictionalized account of the life of Ruth of Moab. I'd start with her childhood in the Chemosh-worshiping Moabite territory, cover her interracial and interfaith marriage, her ten years of infertility, the loss of her husband and his relatives, her conversion, her struggles with an initially ungrateful mother-in-law, her marriage to old-guy Boaz, relations with her new ex-hooker mother-in-law, Rahab, the coronation of her great grandson, David, and her relationship with his wife, Bathsheba. Then I took a breath, and told my friend with a wink that the account might not have enough drama.

You don't actually have to be an expert in ancient Near Eastern history and customs to get a handle on Ruth's story. In *Ebony Moon*, my writing mentor, Dr. Reg Grant, reset the story in modern West Texas. When I picked up Reg's book, I didn't know he was telling Ruth's story. As I read away about this family and grew to care for all the characters, Reg suddenly killed off the father-in-law and both of his sons. I thought perhaps Reg needed some help learning to craft a novel. Nobody starts a book by having half the main characters die! What if *Little Women* started with Beth and Meg croaking? Or Star Wars began with the deaths of Princess Leia and Obi-Wan Kenobi? Not a chance.

Yet, about the time the sister-in-law caught a Greyhound out of town in Reg's tale, I slapped my forehead. *He's recast the story of Ruth!* I realized I'd shoved Reg into a novel-writers' box. Sometimes good stories—the best stories—start with authors breaking the rules.

The story recorded in the Book of Ruth starts with loss upon loss. Consider what we find in the first few verses of chapter one:

There was a famine in the land of Judah. This couple leaves "the house of bread" (Beth-lehem) to find bread elsewhere. The irony! Imagine walking into the grocery store and finding every aisle empty. It's hard for most of us in this country to imagine the fear and pain of going hungry with no prospect of a full stomach.

A man from Bethlehem in Judah went to live as a resident foreigner. How desperate would we have to be to move to another land to quell our hunger?

The man's two sons were Mahlon and Kilion. We may find it difficult to see the loss here until we know "Mahlon" means unhealthy or sickly and "Chilion" means puny or weakly.

Sometime later Naomi's husband Elimelech died. Easy to see the loss there.

Her sons married Moabite women. Naomi's sons married outside of their faith. How would you feel if that happened to you?

They continued to live there about ten years. Though Naomi waited a decade, her sickly sons never announced "You're going to be a grandma!"

Naomi's two sons, Mahlon and Kilion, also died. Losing spouse and children, plunging you into abject poverty? Does it get any worse than that?

T. S. Eliot, the Nobel-Prize-winning poet, wrote, "The end is where we start from." As Ruth's story opens, Naomi's life looks like it has ended, for all intents and purposes. What does she have to live for? Yet if you've read the story you know that her ending is only her beginning. Certainly, these "ends" at the beginning of the story paint a backdrop against which to view Ruth and Naomi getting a new start. And by chapter four we have a happy ending.

What difficulties are you or your loved ones facing? What heartbreak haunts you? It may look as if all hope is lost, as though God has abandoned you, like the Almighty One has plotted to ruin you. Yet with God such hopeless-looking circumstances can mark the start of beginnings that are far beyond what we can imagine.

Can you trust that what looks to you like an ending may be the beginning of something great?

MONDAY: RUTH'S STORY

1. Pray, asking God to give you understanding and insight. Then read the Book of Ruth (below) in one sitting.

Ruth 1

1:1 During the time of the judges there was a famine in the land of Judah. So a man from Bethlehem in Judah went to live as a resident foreigner in the region of Moab, along with his wife and two sons. **1:2** (Now the man's name was Elimelech, his wife was Naomi, and his two sons were Mahlon and Kilion. They were of the clan of Ephrath from Bethlehem in Judah.) They entered the region of Moab and settled there. **1:3** Sometime later Naomi's husband Elimelech died, so she and her two sons were left alone. **1:4** So her sons married Moabite women. (One was named Orpah and the other Ruth.) And they continued to live there about ten years. **1:5** Then Naomi's two sons, Mahlon and Kilion, also died. So the woman was left all alone—bereaved of her two children as well as her husband! **1:6** So she decided to return home from the region of Moab, accompanied by her daughters-in-law, because while she was living in Moab she had heard that the LORD had shown concern for his people, reversing the famine by providing abundant crops.

1:7 Now as she and her two daughters-in-law began to leave the place where she had been living to return to the land of Judah,

1:8 Naomi said to her two daughters-in-law, "Listen to me! Each of you should return to your mother's home! May the LORD show you the same kind of devotion that you have shown to your deceased husbands and to me! **1:9** May the LORD enable each of you to find security in the home of a new husband!" Then she kissed them goodbye and they wept loudly. **1:10** But they said to her, "No! We will return with you to your people."

1:11 But Naomi replied, "Go back home, my daughters! There is no reason for you to return to Judah with me! I am no longer capable of giving birth to sons who might become your husbands! **1:12** Go back home, my daughters! For I am too old to get married again. Even if I thought that there was hope that I could get married tonight and conceive sons, **1:13** surely you would not want to wait until they were old enough to marry! Surely you would not remain unmarried all that time! No, my daughters, you must not return with me. For my intense suffering is too much for you to bear. For the LORD is afflicting me!"

1:14 Again they wept loudly. Then Orpah kissed her mother-in-law goodbye, but Ruth clung tightly to her. **1:15** So Naomi said, "Look, your sister-in-law is returning to her people and to her god. Follow your sister-in-law back home!" **1:16** But Ruth replied,

"Stop urging me to abandon you!

For wherever you go, I will go.

Wherever you live, I will live.

Your people will become my people,

and your God will become my God.

1:17 Wherever you die, I will die—and there I will be buried.

May the LORD punish me severely if I do not keep my promise!

Only death will be able to separate me from you!"

1:18 When Naomi realized that Ruth was determined to go with her, she stopped trying to dissuade her. **1:19** So the two of them journeyed together until they arrived in Bethlehem.

When they entered Bethlehem, the whole village was excited about their arrival. The women of the village said, "Can this be Naomi?" **1:20** But she replied to them, "Don't call me 'Naomi'! Call me 'Mara' because the Sovereign One has treated me very harshly. **1:21** I left here full, but the LORD has caused me to return empty-handed. Why do you call me 'Naomi,' seeing that the LORD has opposed me, and the Sovereign One has caused me to suffer?" **1:22** So Naomi returned, accompanied by her Moabite daughter-in-law

Ruth, who came back with her from the region of Moab. (Now they arrived in Bethlehem at the beginning of the barley harvest.)

Ruth 2

2:1 Now Naomi had a relative on her husband's side of the family named Boaz. He was a wealthy, prominent man from the clan of Elimelech. **2:2** One day Ruth the Moabite said to Naomi, "Let me go to the fields so I can gather grain behind whoever permits me to do so." Naomi replied, "You may go, my daughter." **2:3** So Ruth went and gathered grain in the fields behind the harvesters. Now she just happened to end up in the portion of the field belonging to Boaz, who was from the clan of Elimelech.

2:4 Now at that very moment, Boaz arrived from Bethlehem and greeted the harvesters, "May the LORD be with you!" They replied, "May the LORD bless you!" **2:5** Boaz asked his servant in charge of the harvesters, "To whom does this young woman belong?" **2:6** The servant in charge of the harvesters replied, "She's the young Moabite woman who came back with Naomi from the region of Moab. **2:7** She asked, 'May I follow the harvesters and gather grain among the bundles?' Since she arrived she has been working hard from this morning until now—except for sitting in the resting hut a short time."

2:8 So Boaz said to Ruth, "Listen carefully, my dear! Do not leave to gather grain in another field. You need not go beyond the limits of this field. You may go along beside my female workers. **2:9** Take note of the field where the men are harvesting and follow behind with the female workers. I will tell the men to leave you alone. When you are thirsty, you may go to the water jars and drink some of the water the servants draw."

2:10 Ruth knelt before him with her forehead to the ground and said to him, "Why are you so kind and so attentive to me, even though I am a foreigner?" **2:11** Boaz replied to her, "I have been given a full report of all that you have done for your mother-in-law following the death of your husband—how you left your father and your mother, as well as your homeland, and came to live among people you did not know previously. **2:12** May the LORD reward your efforts! May your acts of kindness be repaid fully by the LORD God of Israel, from whom you have sought protection!" **2:13** She said, "You really are being kind to me, sir, for you have reassured and encouraged me, your servant, even though I am not one of your servants!"

2:14 Later during the mealtime Boaz said to her, "Come here and have some food! Dip your bread in the vinegar!" So she sat down beside the harvesters. Then he handed her some roasted grain. She ate until she was full and saved the rest. **2:15** When she got up to gather grain, Boaz told his male servants, "Let her gather grain even among the bundles! Don't chase her off! **2:16** Make sure you pull out ears of grain for her and drop them so she can gather them up. Don't tell her not to!" **2:17** So she gathered grain in the field until evening. When she threshed what she had gathered, it came to about thirty pounds of barley!

2:18 She carried it back to town, and her mother-in-law saw how much grain she had gathered. Then Ruth gave her the roasted grain she had saved from mealtime. **2:19** Her mother-in-law asked her, "Where did you gather grain today? Where did you work? May the one who took notice of you be rewarded!" So Ruth told her mother-in-law with whom she had worked. She said, "The name of the man with whom I worked today is Boaz." **2:20** Naomi said to her daughter-in-law, "May he be rewarded by the LORD because he has shown loyalty to the living on behalf of the dead!" Then Naomi said to her, "This man is a close relative of ours; he is our guardian." **2:21** Ruth the Moabite replied, "He even told me, 'You may go along beside my servants until they have finished gathering all my harvest!'" **2:22** Naomi then said to her daughter-in-law Ruth, "It is good, my daughter, that you should go out to work with his female servants. That way you will not be harmed, which could happen in another field." **2:23** So Ruth worked beside Boaz's female servants, gathering grain until the end of the barley harvest as well as the wheat harvest. After that she stayed home with her mother-in-law.

3:1 At that time, Naomi, her mother-in-law, said to her, "My daughter, I must find a home for you so you will be secure. **3:2** Now Boaz, with whose female servants you worked, is our close relative. Look, tonight he is winnowing barley at the threshing floor. **3:3** So bathe yourself, rub on some perfumed oil, and get dressed up. Then go down to the threshing floor. But don't let the man know you're there until he finishes his meal. **3:4** When he gets ready to go to sleep, take careful notice of the place where he lies down. Then go, uncover his legs, and lie down beside him. He will tell you what you should do." **3:5** Ruth replied to Naomi, "I will do everything you have told me to do."

3:6 So she went down to the threshing floor and did everything her mother-in-law had instructed her to do. **3:7** When Boaz had finished his meal and was feeling satisfied, he lay down to sleep at the far end of the grain heap. Then Ruth crept up quietly, uncovered his legs, and lay down beside him. **3:8** In the middle of the night he was startled and turned over. Now he saw a woman lying beside him! **3:9** He said, "Who are you?" She replied, "I am Ruth, your servant. Marry your servant, for you are a guardian of the family interests." **3:10** He said, "May you be rewarded by the LORD, my dear! This act of devotion is greater than what you did before. For you have not sought to marry one of the young men, whether rich or poor. **3:11** Now, my dear, don't worry! I intend to do for you everything you propose, for everyone in the village knows that you are a worthy woman. **3:12** Now yes, it is true that I am a guardian, but there is another guardian who is a closer relative than I am. **3:13** Remain here tonight. Then in the morning, if he agrees to marry you, fine, let him do so. But if he does not want to do so, I promise, as surely as the LORD lives, to marry you. Sleep here until morning." **3:14** So she slept beside him until morning. She woke up while it was still dark. Boaz thought, "No one must know that a woman visited the threshing floor." **3:15** Then he said, "Hold out the shawl you are wearing and grip it tightly." As she held it tightly, he measured out about sixty pounds of barley into the shawl and put it on her shoulders. Then he went into town, **3:16** and she returned to her mother-in-law.

When Ruth returned to her mother-in-law, Naomi asked, "How did things turn out for you, my daughter?" Ruth told her about all the man had done for her. **3:17** She said, "He gave me these sixty pounds of barley, for he said to me, 'Do not go to your mother-in-law empty-handed.'" **3:18** Then Naomi said, "Stay put, my daughter, until you know how the matter turns out. For the man will not rest until he has taken care of the matter today."

Ruth 4

4:1 Now Boaz went up to the village gate and sat there. Then along came the guardian whom Boaz had mentioned to Ruth! Boaz said, "Come here and sit down, 'John Doe'!" So he came and sat down. **4:2** Boaz chose ten of the village leaders and said, "Sit down here!" So they sat down. **4:3** Then Boaz said to the guardian, "Naomi, who has returned from the region of Moab, is selling the portion of land that belongs to our relative Elimelech. **4:4** So I am legally informing you: Acquire it before those sitting here and before the leaders of my people! If you want to exercise your right to redeem it, then do so. But if not, then tell me so I will know. For you possess the first option to redeem it; I am next in line after you." He replied, "I will redeem it." **4:5** Then Boaz said, "When you acquire the field from Naomi, you must also acquire Ruth the Moabite, the wife of our deceased relative, in order to preserve his family name by raising up a descendant who will inherit his property." **4:6** The guardian said, "Then I am unable to redeem it, for I would ruin my own inheritance in that case. You may exercise my redemption option, for I am unable to redeem it." **4:7** (Now this used to be the customary way to finalize a transaction involving redemption in Israel: A man would remove his sandal and give it to the other party. This was a legally binding act in Israel.) **4:8** So the guardian said to Boaz, "You may acquire it," and he removed his sandal. **4:9** Then Boaz said to the leaders and all the people, "You are witnesses today that I have acquired from Naomi all that belonged to Elimelech, Kilion, and Mahlon. **4:10** I have also acquired Ruth the Moabite, the wife of Mahlon, as my wife to raise up a descendant who will inherit his property so the name of the deceased might not disappear from among his relatives and from his village. You are witnesses today." **4:11** All the people who were at the gate and the elders replied, "We are witnesses. May the LORD make the woman who is entering your home like Rachel and Leah, both of whom built up the house of Israel! May you prosper in Ephrathah and become famous in Bethlehem. **4:12** May your family become like the family of Perez—whom Tamar bore to Judah—through the descendants the LORD gives you by this young woman."

4:13 So Boaz married Ruth and had sexual relations with her. The LORD enabled her to conceive and she gave birth to a son. **4:14** The village women said to Naomi, "May the LORD be praised because he has not left you without a guardian today! May he become famous in Israel! **4:15** He will encourage you and provide for you when you are old, for your daughter-in-law, who loves you, has given him birth. She is better to you than seven sons!" **4:16** Naomi took the child and placed him on her lap; she became his caregiver. **4:17** The neighbor women named him, saying, "A son has been born to Naomi." They named him Obed. Now he became the father of Jesse—David's father!

4:18 These are the descendants of Perez: Perez was the father of Hezron, **4:19** Hezron was the father of Ram, Ram was the father of Amminadab, **4:20** Amminadab was the father of Nachshon, Nachshon was the father of Salmah, **4:21** Salmon was the father of Boaz, Boaz was the father of Obed, **4:22** Obed was the father of Jesse, and Jesse was the father of David.

2. Write in your own words the gist of the story you've just read:

_____

_____

_____

_____

3. What stands out to you?

_____

_____

_____

_____

4. List circumstances in your life, or in the life of a loved one—particularly difficult circumstances—which, at the time, felt like mere chance, but later you recognized as having been controlled by God in His sovereignty.

_____

_____

_____

_____

_____

1. Read the background information below. It will help you get a context for Ruth's story.

Author—The Bible does not say who wrote the Book of Ruth, or when it was written. The Talmud ascribes authorship to Samuel. Others think the prophet Nathan may have written Ruth during King David's reign. Still others believe it was written during the period when Israel was exiled (after the kings and captivities) to encourage those returning to their homeland.

Time and Setting—By the time the genealogy at the end of Ruth was written, Ruth had become King David's grandmother. So, her story took place two generations before his birth. To understand what was happening in Ruth's time, we need to consider a condensed history of Israel.

Hundreds of years prior to our story, Abram, though childless, had a promise from God that he would become a great nation through whom the whole earth would be blessed. (See Gen. 12.) Abraham's son, Isaac, had a son named Jacob, who had twelve sons and a daughter. One of the twelve sons was Joseph, Jacob's favorite son, who was born to Jacob's favorite wife. You may know his story—Joseph is the one whose father gave him a many-colored coat. Joseph had some dreams about his brothers bowing down to him, which was the proverbial last straw for them. Joseph's brothers, enraged with jealousy, sold their brother into slavery, made up a tale about a vicious animal killing him, and offered his blood-stained coat as proof.

Off in Egypt, the slave Joseph rose to power, but then he was falsely accused of carousing with the wife of Pharaoh's right-hand man. So, Joseph did a lot of time in a dungeon. But then Pharaoh had some dreams and word filtered up the ranks that Joseph could interpret them.

Joseph rightly understood the dreams as signs of coming famine, and he helped Pharaoh take advantage of seven good pre-famine years to prepare. When the famine hit, it scorched the earth as far away as the land where Joseph's family still lived. And Jacob's brothers, having heard Egypt still had food available, left their home and set off to seek food in the land of pyramids. (It's always a bad sign when God's people have to leave Israel due to famine.) The brothers arrived, and kneeling, asked for help, unaware that Joseph was the one before whom they were bowing. Then Joseph, Egypt's second in command, acknowledged God's sovereignty, forgave his brothers, and saved the lives of his family members. (You can read Joseph's entire story in Genesis 30–50.)

Jacob's descendants resettled in Egypt, presumably to wait out the famine, but they ended up staying for centuries. The circumstance of leaving the chosen land to seek food in time of famine will show up again in the Book of Ruth.

One of Joseph's brothers was Judah. Through his line, Messiah was promised.

Over several centuries of power changes in Egypt, Jacob's descendants ended up as slaves. By about five hundred years later, Jacob's descendants were badly oppressed. So God raised up Moses to lead His people out of bondage and into the "promised land," the land God promised Abraham. (You can read Moses' story in the Book of Exodus.)

Succeeding Moses was Joshua. Under Joshua's able leadership, Israel marched into the Promised Land. After many successful military campaigns, the nation of Israel generally subdued the violent, pagan peoples. When Joshua retired after a long, successful career, the nation's future looked fabulous.

Sadly, this situation deteriorated rapidly.

In the years that followed, the Lord led His people through specially-selected leaders called judges. You may be familiar with some of them—Gideon and Deborah and Samson. (You can read about them in the Old Testament book, Judges, or through *Java with the Judges* in the Coffee Cup Bible Study series. The map shows the region where each lived.) Today we might think of a judge as a person who presides in court. Yet judges during this time were often both judicial officials and military leaders or clan chieftains. Two—Deborah and Samuel—were also prophets. Occasionally, these judges appeared in different areas among Israel's tribes, often bringing deliverance from enemies who threatened parts of the nation.

The period of the judges dates from approximately 1220 BC to 1050 BC. My pastor calls the period of judges, as recorded in the Book of Judges, "the General Hospital of the First Testament." Indeed, some deeply flawed leaders, such as Samson, led the nation through one drama after another. The deterioration of the nation is evident in the account of a gang rape at the end of the book of Judges. Yet through their convoluted history, we see once again how the God who made elaborate promises, kept them, despite a nation's continuing rebellion.

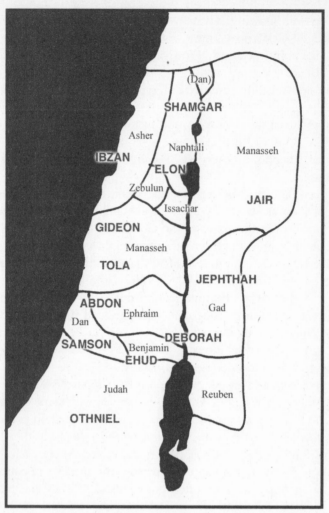

Map of Israel During the Time of the Judges

We also see the lives of some remarkable people, Hannah, Deborah, Jael, and Ruth, who stand out as remarkable women of faith.

The nation reaped the consequences of the Israelites' failure to completely annihilate the Canaanites, as God commanded. Continued disobedience plunged the nation into a downward cycle. First, they sinned. Next, they suffered. Then, they cried out to God, and God delivered them. After that, they sinned again. The cycle looked something like the chart on the next page, with levels of morality plunging deeper each time, until finally the people stop praying and repenting:

During this downward trend in the nation's history, a Gentile girl

The Cycle of Misery

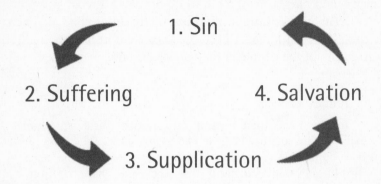

1. Sin

2. Suffering

4. Salvation

3. Supplication

from neighboring Moab, Israel's enemy, arrived on the scene. Her name was Ruth.

Suffering during the period of judges came through famine and war. Yet, one whom the people of Israel might have considered an enemy, a girl from a country with pagan practices that included child sacrifice, shone as a bright light in the dark. She proved more righteous than many who already knew the Lord, and in exercising extraordinary loyalty and kindness, this girl came to worship the Self-Existent One.

Date—No date is given within the Book of Ruth to indicate when it was written. Ruth 1:1 tells us that the events happened "when the judges judged." Perhaps, this is why the book, as we read it today, is placed right after Judges, and that is why we've spent time here establishing what that period was like. It is thought the events in the Book of Ruth probably happened near the end of the Book of Judges. At the earliest, Ruth was completed when David was anointed king; at the latest it was probably written at the end of David's reign, as the book's closing genealogy does not include Solomon. The book's events, then, happened around 1000 BC.

As mentioned, the Book of Ruth was most likely written at the same time as events that fall late in the Book of Judges. So find a comfortable chair, and read Judges 17–21. As you read, note, in particular, the spiritual state of the people in the region of Ephraim and the town of Bethlehem:

Judges 17

Judges 17:1 There was a man named Micah from the Ephraimite hill country. **17:2** He said to his mother, "You know the eleven hundred pieces of silver which were stolen from you, about which I heard you pronounce a curse? Look here, I have the silver. I stole it, but now I am giving it back to you." His mother said, "May the Lord reward you, my son!" **17:3** When he gave back to his mother the eleven hundred pieces of silver, his mother said, "I solemnly dedicate this silver to the Lord. It will be for my son's benefit. We will use it to make a carved image and a metal image." **17:4** When he gave the silver back to his mother, she took two hundred pieces of silver to a silversmith, who made them into a carved image and a metal image. She then put them in Micah's house. **17:5** Now this man Micah owned a shrine. He made an ephod and some personal idols and hired one of his sons to serve as a priest. **17:6** In those days Israel had no king. Each man did what he considered to be right.

17:7 There was a young man from BETHLEHEM in Judah. He was a Levite who had been temporarily residing among the tribe of Judah. **17:8** This man left the town of BETHLEHEM in Judah to find another place to live. He came to the EPHRAIMITE hill country and made his way to Micah's house. **17:9** Micah said to him, "Where do you come from?" He replied, "I am a Levite from BETHLEHEM in Judah. I am looking for a new place to live." **17:10** Micah said to him, "Stay with me. Become my adviser and priest. I will give you ten pieces of silver per year, plus clothes and food." **17:11** So the Levite agreed to stay with the man; the young man was like a son to Micah. **17:12** Micah paid the Levite; the young man became his priest and lived in Micah's house. **17:13** Micah said, "Now I know God will make me rich, because I have this Levite as my priest."

Judges 18

18:1 In those days Israel had no king. And in those days the

Danite tribe was looking for a place to settle, because at that time they did not yet have a place to call their own among the tribes of Israel. **18:2** The Danites sent out from their whole tribe five representatives, capable men from Zorah and Eshtaol, to spy out the land and explore it. They said to them, "Go, explore the land." They came to the EPHRAIMITE hill country and spent the night at Micah's house. **18:3** As they approached Micah's house, they recognized the accent of the young Levite. So they stopped there and said to him, "Who brought you here? What are you doing in this place? What is your business here?" **18:4** He told them what Micah had done for him, saying, "He hired me and I became his priest." **18:5** They said to him, "Seek a divine oracle for us, so we can know if we will be successful on our mission." **18:6** The priest said to them, "Go with confidence. The LORD will be with you on your mission."

18:7 So the five men journeyed on and arrived in Laish. They noticed that the people there were living securely, like the Sidonians do, undisturbed and unsuspecting. No conqueror was troubling them in any way. They lived far from the Sidonians and had no dealings with anyone. **18:8** When the Danites returned to their tribe in Zorah and Eshtaol, their kinsmen asked them, "How did it go?" **18:9** They said, "Come on, let's attack them, for we saw their land and it is very good. You seem lethargic, but don't hesitate to invade and conquer the land. **18:10** When you invade, you will encounter unsuspecting people. The land is wide! God is handing it over to you—a place that lacks nothing on earth!"

18:11 So six hundred Danites, fully armed, set out from Zorah and Eshtaol. **18:12** They went up and camped in Kiriath Jearim in Judah. (To this day that place is called Camp of Dan. It is west of Kiriath Jearim.) **18:13** From there they traveled through the Ephraimite hill country and arrived at Micah's house. **18:14** The five men who had gone to spy out the land of Laish said to their kinsmen, "Do you realize that inside these houses are an ephod, some personal idols, a carved image, and a metal image? Decide now what you want to do." **18:15** They stopped there, went inside the young Levite's house (which belonged to Micah), and asked him how he was doing. **18:16** Meanwhile the six hundred Danites, fully armed, stood at the entrance to the gate. **18:17** The five men who had gone to spy out the land broke in and stole the carved image, the ephod, the personal idols, and the metal image, while the priest was standing at the entrance to the gate with the six hundred fully armed men. **18:18** When these men broke into Micah's house and stole the carved image, the ephod, the personal idols, and the metal image, the priest said to them, "What are you doing?" **18:19** They said to him, "Shut up! Put your hand over your mouth and come with us! You can be our adviser and priest. Wouldn't it be better to be a priest for a whole Israelite tribe than for just one man's family?" **18:20** The priest was happy. He took the ephod, the personal idols, and the carved image and joined the group.

18:21 They turned and went on their way, but they walked behind the children, the cattle, and their possessions. **18:22** After they had gone a good distance from Micah's house, Micah's neighbors gathered together and caught up with the Danites. **18:23** When they called out to the Danites, the Danites turned around and said to Micah, "Why have you gathered together?" **18:24** He said, "You stole my gods that I made, as well as this priest, and then went away. What do I have left? How can you have the audacity to say to me, 'What do you want?'" **18:25** The Danites said to him, "Don't say another word to us, or some very angry men will attack you, and you and your family will die." **18:26** The Danites went on their way; when Micah realized they were too strong to resist, he turned around and went home.

18:27 Now the Danites took what Micah had made, as well as his priest, and came to Laish, where the people were undisturbed and unsuspecting. They struck them down with the sword and burned the city. **18:28** No one came to the rescue because the city was far from Sidon and they had no dealings with anyone. The city was in a valley near Beth Rehob. The Danites rebuilt the city and occupied it. **18:29** They named it Dan after their ancestor, who was one of Israel's sons. But the city's name used to be Laish. **18:30** The Danites worshiped the carved image. Jonathan, descendant of Gershom, son of Moses, and his descendants served as priests for the tribe of Dan until the time of the exile. **18:31** They worshiped Micah's carved image the whole time God's authorized shrine was in Shiloh.

Judges 19

19:1 In those days Israel had no king. There was a Levite living temporarily in the remote region of the Ephraimite hill country. He acquired a concubine from Bethlehem in Judah. **19:2** However, she got angry at him and went home to her father's house in BETHLEHEM in Judah. When she had been there four months, **19:3** her husband came after her, hoping he could convince her to return. He brought with him his servant and a pair of donkeys. When she brought him into her father's house and the girl's father saw him, he greeted him warmly. **19:4** His father-in-law, the girl's father, persuaded him to stay with him for three days, and they ate and drank together, and spent the night there. **19:5** On the fourth day they woke up early and the Levite got ready to leave. But the girl's father said to his son-in-law, "Have a bite to eat for some energy, then you can go." **19:6** So the two of them sat down and had a meal together. Then the girl's father said to the man, "Why not stay another night and have a good time!" **19:7** When the man got ready to leave, his father-in-law convinced him to stay another night. **19:8** He woke up early in the morning on the fifth day so he could leave, but the girl's father said, "Get some energy. Wait until later in the day to leave!" So they ate a meal together. **19:9** When the man got ready to leave with his concubine and his servant, his father-in-law, the girl's father, said to him, "Look! The day is almost over! Stay another night! Since the day is over, stay another night here and have a good time. You can get up early tomorrow and start your trip home." **19:10** But the man did not want to stay another night. He left and traveled as far as Jebus (that is, Jerusalem). He had with him a pair of saddled donkeys and his concubine.

19:11 When they got near Jebus, it was getting quite late and the servant said to his master, "Come on, let's stop at this Jebusite city and spend the night in it." **19:12** But his master said to him, "We should not stop at a foreign city where non-Israelites live. We will travel on to Gibeah." **19:13** He said to his servant, "Come on, we will go into one of the other towns and spend the night in Gibeah or Ramah." **19:14** So they traveled on, and the sun went down when they were near Gibeah in the territory of Benjamin. **19:15** They stopped there and decided to spend the night in Gibeah. They came into the city and sat down in the town square, but no one invited them to spend the night.

19:16 But then an old man passed by, returning at the end of the day from his work in the field. The man was from the EPHRAIMITE hill country; he was living temporarily in Gibeah. (The residents of the town were Benjaminites.) **19:17** When he looked up and saw the traveler in the town square, the old man said, "Where are you heading? Where do you come from?" **19:18** The Levite said to him, "We are traveling from BETHLEHEM in Judah to the remote region of the EPHRAIMITE hill country. That's where I'm from. I had business in BETHLEHEM in Judah, but now I'm heading home. But no one has invited me into their home. **19:19** We have enough straw and grain for our donkeys, and there is enough food and wine for me, your female servant, and the young man who is with your servants. We lack nothing." **19:20** The old man said, "Everything is just fine! I will take care of all your needs. But don't spend the night in the town square." **19:21** So he brought him to his house and fed the donkeys. They washed their feet and had a meal.

19:22 They were having a good time, when suddenly some men of the city, some good-for-nothings, surrounded the house and kept beating on the door. They said to the old man who owned the house, "Send out the man who came to visit you so we can have sex with him." **19:23** The man who owned the house went outside and said to them, "No, my brothers! Don't do this wicked thing! After all, this man is a guest in my house. Don't do such a disgraceful thing! **19:24** Here are my virgin daughter and my guest's concubine. I will send them out and you can abuse them and do to them whatever you like. But don't do such a disgraceful thing to this man!" **19:25** The men refused to listen to him, so the Levite grabbed his concubine and made her go outside. They raped her and abused her all night long until morning. They let her go at dawn. **19:26** The woman arrived back at daybreak and was sprawled out on the doorstep of the house where her master was staying until it became light. **19:27** When her master got up in the morning, opened the doors of the house, and went outside to start on his journey, there was the woman, his concubine, sprawled out on the doorstep of the house with her hands on the threshold. **19:28** He said to her, "Get up, let's leave!" But there was no response. He put her on the donkey and went home. **19:29** When he got home, he took a knife, grabbed his concubine, and carved her up into twelve pieces. Then he sent the pieces throughout Israel. **19:30** Everyone who saw the sight said, "Nothing like this has happened or been witnessed during the entire time since the Israelites left the land of Egypt! Take careful note of it! Discuss it and speak!"

Judges 20

20:1 All the Israelites from Dan to Beer Sheba and from the land of Gilead left their homes and assembled together before the LORD at Mizpah. **20:2** The leaders of all the people from all the tribes of Israel took their places in the assembly of God's people, which numbered four hundred thousand sword-wielding foot soldiers. **20:3** The Benjaminites heard that the Israelites had gone up to Mizpah. Then the Israelites said, "Explain how this wicked thing happened!" **20:4** The Levite, the husband of the murdered woman, spoke up, "I and my concubine stopped in Gibeah in the territory of Benjamin to spend the night. **20:5** The leaders of Gibeah attacked me and at night surrounded the house where I was staying. They wanted to kill me; instead they abused my concubine so badly that she died. **20:6** I grabbed hold of my concubine and carved her up and sent the pieces throughout the territory occupied by Israel, because they committed such an unthinkable atrocity in Israel. 20:7 All you Israelites, make a decision here!"

20:8 All Israel rose up in unison and said, "Not one of us will go home! Not one of us will return to his house! **20:9** Now this is what we will do to Gibeah: We will attack the city as the lot dictates. **20:10** We will take ten of every group of a hundred men from all the tribes of Israel (and a hundred of every group of a thousand, and a thousand of every group of ten thousand) to get supplies for the army. When they arrive in Gibeah of Benjamin they will punish them for the atrocity which they committed in Israel." **20:11** So all the men of Israel gathered together at the city as allies.

20:12 The tribes of Israel sent men throughout the tribe of Benjamin, saying, "How could such a wicked thing take place? **20:13** Now, hand over the good-for-nothings in Gibeah so we can execute them and purge Israel of wickedness." But the Benjaminites refused to listen to their Israelite brothers. **20:14** The Benjaminites came from their cities and assembled at Gibeah to make war against the Israelites. **20:15** That day the Benjaminites mustered from their cities twenty-six thousand sword-wielding soldiers, besides seven hundred well-trained soldiers from Gibeah. **20:16** Among this army were seven hundred specially-trained left-handed soldiers. Each one could sling a stone and hit even the smallest target. **20:17** The men of Israel (not counting Benjamin) had mustered four hundred thousand sword-wielding soldiers, every one an experienced warrior.

20:18 The Israelites went up to Bethel and asked God, "Who should lead the charge against the Benjaminites?" The LORD said, "Judah should lead." **20:19** The Israelites got up the next morning and moved against Gibeah. **20:20** The men of Israel marched out to fight Benjamin; they arranged their battle lines against Gibeah. **20:21** The Benjaminites attacked from Gibeah and struck down twenty-two thousand Israelites that day.

20:22 The Israelite army took heart and once more arranged their battle lines, in the same place where they had taken their positions the day before. **20:23** The Israelites went up and wept before the LORD until evening. They asked the LORD, "Should we again march out to fight the Benjaminites, our brothers?" The LORD said, "Attack them!" **20:24** So the Israelites marched toward the Benjaminites the next day. **20:25** The Benjaminites again attacked them from Gibeah and struck down eighteen thousand sword-wielding Israelite soldiers.

20:26 So all the Israelites, the whole army, went up to Bethel.

They wept and sat there before the LORD; they did not eat anything that day until evening. They offered up burnt sacrifices and tokens of peace to the LORD. **20:27** The Israelites asked the LORD (for the ark of God's covenant was there in those days; **20:28** Phinehas son of Eleazar, son of Aaron, was serving the LORD in those days), "Should we once more march out to fight the Benjaminites our brothers, or should we quit?" The LORD said, "Attack, for tomorrow I will hand them over to you."

20:29 So Israel hid men in ambush outside Gibeah. **20:30** The Israelites attacked the Benjaminites the next day; they took their positions against Gibeah just as they had done before. **20:31** The Benjaminites attacked the army, leaving the city unguarded. They began to strike down their enemy just as they had done before. On the main roads (one leads to Bethel, the other to Gibeah) and in the field, they struck down about thirty Israelites. **20:32** Then the Benjaminites said, "They are defeated just as before." But the Israelites said, "Let's retreat and lure them away from the city into the main roads." **20:33** All the men of Israel got up from their places and took their positions at Baal Tamar, while the Israelites hiding in ambush jumped out of their places west of Gibeah. **20:34** Ten thousand men, well-trained soldiers from all Israel, then made a frontal assault against Gibeah—the battle was fierce. But the Benjaminites did not realize that disaster was at their doorstep. **20:35** The LORD annihilated Benjamin before Israel; the Israelites struck down that day 25,100 sword-wielding Benjaminites. **20:36** Then the Benjaminites saw they were defeated.

The Israelites retreated before Benjamin, because they had confidence in the men they had hid in ambush outside Gibeah. **20:37** The men hiding in ambush made a mad dash to Gibeah. They attacked and put the sword to the entire city. **20:38** The Israelites and the men hiding in ambush had arranged a signal. When the men hiding in ambush sent up a smoke signal from the city, **20:39** the Israelites counterattacked. Benjamin had begun to strike down the Israelites; they struck down about thirty men. They said, "There's no doubt about it! They are totally defeated as in the earlier battle." **20:40** But when the signal, a pillar of smoke, began to rise up from the city, the Benjaminites turned around and saw the whole city going up in a cloud of smoke that rose high into the sky. **20:41** When the Israelites turned around, the Benjaminites panicked because they could see that disaster was on their doorstep. **20:42** They retreated before the Israelites, taking the road to the wilderness. But the battle overtook them as men from the surrounding cities struck them down. **20:43** They surrounded the Benjaminites, chased them from Nohah, and annihilated them all the way to a spot east of Geba. **20:44** Eighteen thousand Benjaminites, all of them capable warriors, fell dead. **20:45** The rest turned and ran toward the wilderness, heading toward the cliff of Rimmon. But the Israelites caught five thousand of them on the main roads. They stayed right on their heels all the way to Gidom and struck down two thousand more. **20:46** That day twenty-five thousand sword-wielding Benjaminites fell in battle, all of them capable warriors. **20:47** Six hundred survivors turned and ran away to the wilderness, to the cliff of Rimmon. They stayed there four months. **20:48** The Israelites returned to the Benjaminite towns and put the sword to them. They wiped out the cities, the animals, and everything they could find. They set fire to every city in their path.

Judges 21

21:1 The Israelites had taken an oath in Mizpah, saying, "Not one of us will allow his daughter to marry a Benjaminite." **21:2** So the people came to Bethel and sat there before God until evening, weeping loudly and uncontrollably. **21:3** They said, "Why, O LORD God of Israel, has this happened in Israel? An entire tribe has disappeared from Israel today!"

21:4 The next morning the people got up early and built an altar there. They offered up burnt sacrifices and token[s] of peace. **21:5** The Israelites asked, "Who from all the Israelite tribes has not assembled before the LORD?" They had made a solemn oath that whoever did not assemble before the LORD at Mizpah must certainly be executed. **21:6** The Israelites regretted what had happened to their brother Benjamin. They said, "Today we cut off an entire tribe from Israel! **21:7** How can we find wives for those who are left? After all, we took an oath in the LORD's name not to give them our daughters as wives." **21:8** So they asked, "Who from all the Israelite tribes did not assemble before the LORD at Mizpah?" Now it just so happened no one from Jabesh Gilead had come to the gathering. **21:9** When they took roll call, they noticed none of the inhabitants of Jabesh Gilead were there. **21:10** So the assembly sent 12,000 capable warriors against Jabesh Gilead. They commanded them, "Go and kill with your swords the inhabitants of Jabesh Gilead, including the women and little children. **21:11** Do this: exterminate every male, as well as every woman who has had sexual relations with a male. But spare the lives of any virgins." So they did as instructed. **21:12** They found among the inhabitants of

Jabesh Gilead four hundred young girls who were virgins—they had never had sexual relations with a male. They brought them back to the camp at Shiloh in the land of Canaan.

21:13 The entire assembly sent messengers to the Benjaminites at the cliff of Rimmon and assured them they would not be harmed. **21:14** The Benjaminites returned at that time, and the Israelites gave to them the women they had spared from Jabesh Gilead. But there were not enough to go around.

21:15 The people regretted what had happened to Benjamin because the LORD had weakened the Israelite tribes. **21:16** The leaders of the assembly said, "How can we find wives for those who are left? After all, the Benjaminite women have been wiped out. **21:17** The remnant of Benjamin must be preserved. An entire Israelite tribe should not be wiped out. **21:18** But we can't allow our daughters to marry them, for the Israelites took an oath, saying, 'Whoever gives a woman to a Benjaminite will be destroyed!' **21:19** However, there is an annual festival to the LORD in Shiloh, which is north of Bethel (east of the main road that goes up from Bethel to Shechem) and south of Lebonah." **21:20** So they commanded the Benjaminites, "Go hide in the vineyards, **21:21** and keep your eyes open. When you see the daughters of Shiloh coming out to dance in the celebration, jump out from the vineyards. Each one of you, catch yourself a wife from among the daughters of Shiloh and then go home to the land of Benjamin. **21:22** When their fathers or brothers come and protest to us, we'll say to them, "Do us a favor and let them be, for we could not get each one a wife through battle. Don't worry about breaking your oath! You would only be guilty if you had voluntarily given them wives."

21:23 The Benjaminites did as instructed. They abducted two hundred of the dancing girls to be their wives. They went home to their own territory, rebuilt their cities, and settled down. **21:24** Then the Israelites dispersed from there to their respective tribal and clan territories. Each went from there to his own property. **21:25** In those days Israel had no king. Each man did what he considered to be right.

2. What is your impression of the spiritual climate in Bethlehem at the time these events happened?

_____

_____

3. Contrast the shame in Bethlehem in the above section of Judges with the account in the Book of Ruth of the righteous in Bethlehem:

> **Ruth 1:1** During the time of the judges there was a famine in the land of Judah. So a man from Bethlehem in Judah went to live as a resident foreigner in the region of Moab, along with his wife and two sons. **1:2** (Now the man's name was Elimelech, his wife was Naomi, and his two sons were Mahlon and Kilion. They were of the clan of Ephrath from **Bethlehem** in Judah.) They entered the region of Moab and settled there. **1:3** Sometime later Naomi's husband Elimelech died, so she and her two sons were left alone. **1:4** So her sons married Moabite women. (One was named Orpah and the other Ruth.) And they continued to live there about ten years. **1:5** Then Naomi's two sons, Mahlon and Kilion, also died. So the woman was left all alone—bereaved of her two children as well as her husband! **1:6** So she decided to return home from the region of Moab, accompanied by her daughters-in-law, because while she was living in Moab she had heard that the Lord had shown concern for his people, reversing the famine by providing abundant crops.

* * *

> **1:18** When Naomi realized that Ruth was determined to go with her, she stopped trying to dissuade her. **1:19** So the two of them journeyed together until they arrived in **Bethlehem**. When they entered **Bethlehem**, the whole village was excited about their arrival. The women of the village said, "Can this be Naomi?" **1:20** But she replied to them, "Don't call me 'Naomi'! Call me 'Mara' because the Sovereign One has treated me very harshly. **1:21** I left here full, but the Lord has caused me to return empty-handed. Why do you call me 'Naomi', seeing that the Lord has opposed me, and the Sovereign One has caused me to suffer?" **1:22** So Naomi returned, accompanied by her Moabite daughter-in-law Ruth, who came back with her from the region of Moab. (Now they arrived in **Bethlehem** at the beginning of the barley harvest.)

* * *

> **2:4** Now at that very moment, Boaz arrived from **Bethlehem** and greeted the harvesters, "May the Lord be with you!" They

replied, "May the Lord bless you!" **2:5** Boaz asked his servant in charge of the harvesters, "To whom does this young woman belong?" **2:6** The servant in charge of the harvesters replied, "She's the young Moabite woman who came back with Naomi from the region of Moab. **2:7** She asked, 'May I follow the harvesters and gather grain among the bundles?' Since she arrived she has been working hard from this morning until now—except for sitting in the resting hut a short time."

* * *

4:10 I have also acquired Ruth the Moabite, the wife of Mahlon, as my wife to raise up a descendant who will inherit his property so the name of the deceased might not disappear from among his relatives and from his village. You are witnesses today." **4:11** All the people who were at the gate and the elders replied, "We are witnesses. May the Lord make the woman who is entering your home like Rachel and Leah, both of whom built up the house of Israel! May you prosper in Ephrathah and become famous in **Bethlehem. 4:12** May your family become like the family of Perez— whom Tamar bore to Judah—through the descendants the Lord gives you by this young woman."

4:13 So Boaz married Ruth and had sexual relations with her. The Lord enabled her to conceive and she gave birth to a son. **4:14** The village women said to Naomi, "May the Lord be praised because he has not left you without a guardian today! May he become famous in Israel! **4:15** He will encourage you and provide for you when you are old, for your daughter-in-law, who loves you, has given him birth. She is better to you than seven sons!" **4:16** Naomi took the child and placed him on her lap; she became his caregiver. **4:17** The neighbor women named him, saying, "A son has been born to Naomi." They named him Obed. Now he became the father of Jesse—David's father!

4. What differences did you see between what's highlighted in the Book of Judges and what's capitalized in the Book of Ruth relating to events in Bethlehem?

_____

_____

_____

_____

_____

THURSDAY: OF CULTURAL RELEVANCE

1. Now that we have some background on what was happening in Israel, let's consider the land of Ruth's birth, Moab, and its relationship to Israel. The name "Moab" sounds like Hebrew for the phrase "from father." That fits with the nation's origins:

> **Gen 19:36–37** So both of Lot's daughters became pregnant by their father. The older daughter had a son, and she named him Moab; he is the father of the Moabites of today.

According to Genesis, who was Moab?

_____

_____

_____

2. Now, read Numbers 22-23 to see how Moab treats the Isrealites upon their return from Egypt:

> **Numbers 22:1** The Israelites traveled on and camped in the plains of Moab on the side of the Jordan River across from Jericho. **22:2** Balak son of Zippor saw all that the Israelites had done to the Amorites. **22:3** And the Moabites were greatly afraid of the people, because they were so numerous. The Moabites were sick with fear because of the Israelites.
>
> **22:4** So the Moabites said to the elders of Midian, "Now this mass of people will lick up everything around us, as the bull devours the grass of the field. Now Balak son of Zippor was king of the Moabites at this time. **22:5** And he sent messengers to Balaam son of Beor at Pethor, which is by the Euphrates River in the land of

Amaw, to summon him, saying, "Look, a nation has come out of Egypt. They cover the face of the earth, and they are settling next to me. **22:6** So now, please come and curse this nation for me, for they are too powerful for me. Perhaps I will prevail so that we may conquer them and drive them out of the land. For I know that whoever you bless is blessed, and whoever you curse is cursed."

22:7 So the elders of Moab and the elders of Midian departed with the fee for divination in their hand. They came to Balaam and reported to him the words of Balak. **22:8** He replied to them, "Stay here tonight, and I will bring back to you whatever word the LORD may speak to me." So the princes of Moab stayed with Balaam. **22:9** And God came to Balaam and said, "Who are these men with you?" **22:10** Balaam said to God, "Balak son of Zippor, king of Moab, has sent a message to me, saying, **22:11** "Look, a nation has come out of Egypt, and it covers the face of the earth. Come now and put a curse on them for me; perhaps I will be able to defeat them and drive them out." **22:12** But God said to Balaam, "You must not go with them; you must not curse the people, for they are blessed."

22:13 So Balaam got up in the morning, and said to the princes of Balak, "Go to your land, for the LORD has refused to permit me to go with you." **22:14** So the princes of Moab departed and went back to Balak and said, "Balaam refused to come with us."

22:15 Balak again sent princes, more numerous and more distinguished than the first. **22:16** And they came to Balaam and said to him, "Thus says Balak son of Zippor: 'Please do not let anything hinder you from coming to me. **22:17** For I will honor you greatly, and whatever you tell me I will do. So come, put a curse on this nation for me.'"

22:18 Balaam replied to the servants of Balak, "Even if Balak would give me his palace full of silver and gold, I could not transgress the commandment of the LORD my God to do less or more. **22:19** Now therefore, please stay the night here also, that I may know what more the LORD might say to me." **22:20** God came to Balaam that night, and said to him, "If the men have come to call you, get up and go with them; but the word that I will say to you, that you must do." **22:21** So Balaam got up in the morning, saddled his donkey, and went with the princes of Moab.

22:22 Then God's anger was kindled because he went, and the angel of the LORD stood in the road to oppose him. Now he was riding on his donkey and his two servants were with him. **22:23** And the donkey saw the angel of the LORD standing in the road with his sword drawn in his hand, so the donkey turned aside from the road and went into the field. But Balaam beat the donkey, to make her turn back to the road.

22:24 Then the angel of the LORD stood in a path among the vineyards, where there was a wall on either side. **22:25** And when the donkey saw the angel of the LORD, she pressed herself into the wall, and crushed Balaam's foot against the wall. So he beat her again.

22:26 Then the angel of the LORD went farther, and stood in a narrow place, where there was no way to turn either to the right or to the left. **22:27** When the donkey saw the angel of the LORD, she crouched down under Balaam. Then Balaam was angry, and he beat his donkey with a staff.

22:28 Then the LORD opened the mouth of the donkey, and she said to Balaam, "What have I done to you that you have beaten me these three times?" **22:29** And Balaam said to the donkey, "You have made me look stupid; I wish there were a sword in my hand, for I would kill you right now." **22:30** The donkey said to Balaam, "Am not I your donkey that you have ridden ever since I was yours until this day? Have I ever attempted to treat you this way?" And he said, "No." **22:31** Then the LORD opened Balaam's eyes, and he saw the angel of the LORD standing in the way with his sword drawn in his hand; so he bowed his head and threw himself down with his face to the ground. **22:32** The angel of the LORD said to him, "Why have you beaten your donkey these three times? Look, I came out to oppose you because what you are doing is perverse before me. **22:33** The donkey saw me and turned from me these three times. If she had not turned from me, I would have killed you but saved her alive." **22:34** Balaam said to the angel of the LORD, "I have sinned, for I did not know that you stood against me in the road. So now, if it is evil in your sight, I will go back home." **22:35** But the angel of the LORD said to Balaam, "Go with the men, but you may only speak the word that I will speak to you." So Balaam went with the princes of Balak.

22:36 When Balak heard that Balaam was coming, he went out to meet him at a city of Moab which was on the border of the Arnon at the boundary of his territory. **22:37** Balak said to Balaam, "Did I not send again and again to you to summon you? Why did you not come to me? Am I not able to honor you?" **22:38** Balaam said to Balak, "Look, I have come to you. Now, am I able to speak just anything? I must speak only the word that God puts in my mouth." **22:39** So Balaam went with Balak, and they came to Kiriath-huzoth. **22:40** And Balak sacrificed bulls and sheep, and sent some to Balaam, and to the princes who were with him. **22:41** Then on the next morning Balak took Balaam, and brought him up to Bamoth Baal. From there he saw the extent of the nation.

23:1 Balaam said to Balak, "Build me seven altars here, and prepare for me here seven bulls and seven rams." **23:2** So Balak did just as Balaam had said. Balak and Balaam then offered on each altar a bull and a ram. **23:3** Balaam said to Balak, "Station yourself by your burnt offering, and I will go off; perhaps the LORD will come to meet me, and whatever he reveals to me I will tell you." Then he went to a deserted height.

23:4 Then God met Balaam, who said to him, "I have prepared seven altars, and I have offered on each altar a bull and a ram." **23:5** Then the LORD put a message in Balaam's mouth and said, "Return to Balak, and speak what I tell you."

23:6 So he returned to him, and he was still standing by his burnt offering, he and all the princes of Moab. **23:7** Then Balaam uttered his oracle, saying,

"Balak, the king of Moab, brought me from Aram,

out of the mountains of the east, saying,

'Come, pronounce a curse on Jacob for me;

come, denounce Israel.'

23:8 How can I curse one whom God has not cursed,

or how can I denounce one whom the LORD has not denounced?

23:9 For from the top of the rocks I see them;

from the hills I watch them.

Indeed, a nation that lives alone,

and it will not be reckoned among the nations.

23:10 Who can count the dust of Jacob,

Or number the fourth part of Israel?

Let me die the death of the upright,

and let the end of my life be like theirs."

23:11 Then Balak said to Balaam, "What have you done to me? I brought you to curse my enemies, but on the contrary you have only blessed them!" **23:12** Balaam replied, "Must I not be careful to speak what the LORD has put in my mouth?" **23:13** Balak said to him, "Please come with me to another place from which you can observe them. You will see only a part of them, but you will not see all of them. Curse them for me from there."

23:14 So Balak brought Balaam to the field of Zophim, to the top of Pisgah, where he built seven altars and offered a bull and a ram on each altar. **23:15** And Balaam said to Balak, "Station yourself here by your burnt offering, while I meet the LORD there. **23:16** Then the LORD met Balaam and put a message in his mouth and said, "Return to Balak, and speak what I tell you." **23:17** When Balaam came to him, he was still standing by his burnt offering, along with the princes of Moab. And Balak said to him, "What has the LORD spoken?"

23:18 Balaam uttered his oracle, and said,

"Rise up, Balak, and hear;

Listen to me, son of Zippor:

23:19 God is not a man, that he should lie,

nor a human being, that he should change his mind.

Has he said, and will he not do it?

Or has he spoken, and will he not make it happen?

23:20 Indeed, I have received a command to bless;

he has blessed, and I cannot reverse it.

23:21 He has not looked on iniquity in Jacob,

nor has he seen trouble in Israel.

The LORD their God is with them;

his acclamation as king is among them.

23:22 God brought them out of Egypt.

They have, as it were, the strength of a wild bull.

23:23 For there is no spell against Jacob,

nor is there any divination against Israel.

At this time it must be said of Jacob

and of Israel, 'Look at what God has done!'

23:24 Indeed, the people will rise up like a lioness,

and like a lion raises himself up;

they will not lie down until they eat their prey,

and drink the blood of the slain."

23:25 Balak said to Balaam, "Neither curse them at all nor bless them at all!"

23:26 But Balaam replied to Balak, "Did I not tell you, 'All that the LORD speaks, I must do'?"

23:27 Balak said to Balaam, "Come, please; I will take you to another place. Perhaps it will please God to let you curse them for me from there." **23:28** So Balak took Balaam to the top of Peor, that looks toward the wilderness. **23:29** Then Balaam said to Balak, "Build seven altars here for me, and prepare seven bulls and seven rams." **23:30** So Balak did as Balaam had said, and offered a bull and a ram on each altar.

3. How did Moab (as a nation) respond when the children of Israel were returning from Egypt?

_____

_____

_____

_____

_____

4. The people of Moab worshiped Chemosh, a false god.

Numbers 21:29 says this:

"Woe to you, O Moab! You are destroyed, O people of Chemosh! He has given up his sons as fugitives and his daughters as captives to Sihon king of the Amorites."

Years after Ruth's story, 2 Kings 3:26–27 records this:

"When the king of Moab saw that the battle had gone against him, he took with him seven hundred swordsmen to break through to the king of Edom, but they failed. Then he took his firstborn son, who was to succeed him as king, and offered him as a sacrifice on the city wall. The fury against Israel was great; they withdrew and returned to their own land."

Deut. 23:3–4 gives us a good idea about how God felt about Moab:

Deuteronomy 23:3 No Ammonite or Moabite or any of his descendants may enter the assembly of the LORD, even down to the tenth generation. **23:4** For they did not come to meet you with bread and water on your way when you came out of Egypt, and they hired Balaam son of Beor from Pethor in Aram Naharaim to pronounce a curse on you.

Summarize what you've just read. What were Moab's religious loyalties? How do you think God viewed the Moabites? Why?

_____

_____

_____

_____

_____

Based on what you've just read, how do you think we should interpret the fact that Naomi's family left Bethlehem to go to Moab and that her two sons married Moabite girls? Was it an act of faith or disobedience or neither?

_____

_____

_____

_____

FRIDAY: CAST AND CUSTOM

1. Now that you have read the story, let's get more familiar with its main characters:

Elimelech—The name means "My God is King." Where was he from, according to Ruth 1:2?

_____

Mahlon and Kilion—All we know about these two men, other than the names of their parents and wives, is what their names mean—sickly and weakly.

Naomi—Naomi's name means "pleasant." Later she renamed herself "Mara," which means "bitter."

Orpah—"Orpah" means "deer" or "fawn." According to rabbinic literature, Orpah is identified with Harafa, who gave birth to four Philistine giants. Legend has it that these four sons were given her for the four tears she shed at parting with Naomi.[1] According to a midrash—an early Jewish commentary on a biblical text—Orpah was actually Ruth's sister, and both were daughters of the Moabite king Eglon.[2] Her name was changed to "Orpah" because she turned her back on her mother-in-law.[3] One Talmudic source says she was killed years later by King David's general Abishai, the son of Zeruiah.[4] If so, she lived to be a very old woman, as by then Ruth would have given birth to Obed, who would have grown up to have a son named Jesse, whose youngest was David, who had to grow up before having a general! Trivia: If Oprah Winfrey's name looks similar to Orpah's, it's because Oprah was supposed to be named for her, but apparently the birth certificate arrived with a typo (Oprah says her mother didn't know how to spell Orpah). Had it arrived as intended, Oprah's company would be called "Hapro Productions" rather than "Harpo Productions."

E. Ruth—Ruth's name means "friend." She was married to sickly Mahlon for a decade before he died, leaving her childless. She is mentioned in the Bible only in the book bearing her name and in the genealogy of Jesus (Matt. 1:5). Born in Moab, she married an Israelite. She left her gods and her parents to go with a penniless, grieving mother-in-law to the home of her deceased husband. In providing for an old, unhappy woman, Ruth shows great loyal love and ends up being an ancestress in David's line, and ultimately Jesus Christ's.

F. Boaz—Boaz, meaning "quick" or "swiftness," lived in Bethlehem. "Beth" means "house and "lehem" means "bread." ("Beth-el" means "house of God.") The son of Rahab and a relative of Naomi's deceased husband, Boaz was called a *gibbor hayil* (Ruth 2:1). The phrase can be translated either "a mighty man of valor" or "a man of position and wealth." The phrase as used to describe Boaz in the Book of Ruth appears to emphasize economic stature rather than warrior status.

[1] Babylonian Talmud, Sotah 42b
[2] Ruth R. ii. 9.
[3] Babylonian Talmud, Sotah lc
[4] Sanhedrin 95a

Boaz married Ruth, and their son, Obed, was the father of Jesse, father of David (the king). According to 1 Chronicles 2:11–12, Boaz descended from Hezron, which means Boaz was likely a chief of Hezron's clan in Bethlehem. The historian Josephus said the judge, Ibzan, was from Bethlehem[5], Boaz's town. And the Talmud identifies Boaz with the Ibzan named in the book of Judges[6]: "Ibzan of Bethlehem led Israel. He had thirty sons. He arranged for thirty of his daughters to be married outside his extended family, and he arranged for thirty young women to be brought from outside as wives for his sons. Ibzan led Israel for seven years; then he died and was buried in Bethlehem" (Judges 12:8–10).

Five generations after Boaz, Solomon built his great temple. One of its bronze pillars bore the same three consonants that make up Boaz's name. (There is no way to show this in English, since "Boaz" has only two consonants, but it would be similar to writing Mrk for Mark. Like "Boaz" in Hebrew, in English "Mark" can be both proper name and symbol.) Depending on how one fills in the vowels (Mark, Mork, Mirk), which the Hebrew of the time didn't have, the inscription refers to a man named Boaz or it means "in strength." So the temple's Pillar of Boaz could have honored Boaz in the Book of Ruth;

---

[5] Flavius Josephus, *Antiquities*, V, vii, 13. " Now when Jephtha was dead, Ibzan took the government, being of the tribe of Judah, and of the city of Bethlehem. He had sixty children, thirty of them sons, and the rest daughters; all whom he left alive behind him, giving the daughters in marriage to husbands, and taking wives for his sons. He did nothing in the seven years of his administration that was worth recording, or deserved a memorial. So he died an old man, and was buried in his own country."

[6] The Talmud is a compilation of Jewish oral law, which discusses law, ethics, history and customs. It has two components: the Mishnah and Germara. Bava Batra in the Talmud, The Last Gate Chapter 5, says, "The rabbis taught: One must not emigrate from Palestine to other provinces, unless the price of grain has increased to the extent of a selah for two saahs. Said R. Simeon: This is only when one could not find any grain at all to buy; but if he can get it even at the price of a selah for each saah, one must not emigrate. And so also was the opinion of R. Simeon b. Johai, who used to say that Elimelech, Mahlon, and Kilyon were the great men of their generation, and were their leaders; and they were punished only because they emigrated from Palestine. As it is written [Ruth, i. 19]: "All the city was in commotion about them, and people said, "Is this Naomi?" And to the question: What does it mean? said R. Itz'hak: It means: See what has become of Naomi, who emigrated from Palestine. He said again: At that day when Ruth reached Palestine, the wife of Boaz had died; and this is what people say, that before the deceased departed the substitute for managing the house was already prepared. Rabba b. R. Huna in the name of Rabh said: Boaz is identical with Ibzan. . . .That which was said in his name elsewhere, viz.: One hundred and twenty banquets Boaz made for his children. As it is written [Judges, xii. 9]: "And he had thirty sons, and thirty daughters he sent abroad, and thirty daughters he brought in for his sons from abroad," etc. And at each marriage two banquets were given—one in the father's and one in the father-in-law's house—and to not one of them did he invite Manoah, saying: What return can I expect of this childless man?

or honored Boaz, a temple architect or donor; or is not a name at all, but means "strong" and describes the pillar itself: "Pillar of Strength"[7]

2. Now that you're familiar with the main characters, let's consider a specific Israelite custom that helps us understand what's happening in Ruth's story. Read Deuteronomy 25:5–10:

> If brothers live together and one of them dies without having a son, the dead man's wife must not remarry to a stranger, outside the family. Instead, her late husband's brother must go to her, marry her, and perform the duty of a brother-in-law. Then the first son she bears will continue the name of the dead brother, thus preventing his name from being blotted out of Israel. But if the man does not want to marry his brother's widow, then she must go to the elders at the gate and say, "My husband's brother refuses to preserve his brother's name in Israel; he is unwilling to perform the duty of a brother-in-law to me." Then the elders of his city must summon him and speak to him. If he persists, saying, "I don't want to marry her," then his sister-in-law must approach him in view of the elders, remove his sandal from his foot, and spit in his face. She will then respond, "Thus may it be done to any man who does not maintain his brother's lineage." His family name will be recorded in Israel as "the family of the one whose sandal was removed."

"Levirate" is Latin for "brother-in-law," and in this section of Deuteronomy we see what is commonly referred to as instruction on "levirate marriage." What was supposed to happen when a man died without leaving an heir?

_____

_____

_____

_____

_____

And there is a Boraitha that all the children died when he (Boaz) was still alive. And he remarried and begat one who was better than all the sixty, the same was Obed, who was born by Ruth, from whom David descended.

[7] F. Brown, S. Driver, and C. Briggs. *Brown-Driver-Briggs Hebrew and English Lexicon.* Peabody, MA: Hendrickson, 2000, p. 126–127.

3. What happened to Ruth's husband, brother-in-law, and father-in-law according to Ruth 1:4–5?

> **1:4** So her sons married Moabite women. (One was named Orpah and the other Ruth.) And they continued to live there about ten years. **1:5** Then Naomi's two sons, Mahlon and Kilion, also died. So the woman was left all alone—bereaved of her two children as well as her husband!

_____

_____

_____

_____

4. Read Ruth 1:12–13. Now that you know more about levirate law, summarize your understanding of what Naomi was telling her daughters-in-law.

> **1:12** Go back home, my daughters! For I am too old to get married again. Even if I thought that there was hope that I could get married tonight and conceive sons, **1:13** surely you would not want to wait until they were old enough to marry! Surely you would not remain unmarried all that time! No, my daughters, you must not return with me. For my intense suffering is too much for you to bear. For the LORD is afflicting me!"

_____

_____

_____

_____

_____

The events in the Book of Ruth happened about three thousand years ago. Interestingly, when polygamy was abolished in the ancient Near East more than a thousand years ago, Jewish law determined that levirate marriage should also no longer be practiced.[8] Apparently, levirate marriage and polygamy were frequently linked. While we have nothing like levirate marriage in the West, in some cultures, such as tribal groups in Zambia, it is still practiced. And in the Old Testament, God commanded it. He even killed Onan for refusing to contribute to his brother's legacy by impregnating his widow, Tamar (Gen. 38:10). That story will become significant later in our study of Ruth, as Tamar's child, Perez, is in the lineage of Boaz.

While we know from Ephesians 5 that God's ideal for marriage is a monogamous, one-flesh relationship that pictures Christ and the church, levirate marriage was very important to Him as a way of showing loyal love to the deceased.

SATURDAY: THE APRIL/DECEMBER MATCH

> Ruth 1:3–5 "Elimelech, Naomi's husband, died; she and her two sons were left alone. Her sons married Moabite girls. (One was named Orpah and the other Ruth.) They lived there for about ten years. Then Naomi's two sons, Mahlon and Kilion, also died. The woman was left without her two children and her husband."

Ruth and her first husband were childless after ten years of marriage. Imagine, in a culture that valued huge families and in which the only contraception was *coitus interruptus,* or "withdrawal," Ruth was married a decade without conceiving. Something was clearly wrong.

Then her husband and his brother and father died, leaving Ruth with only her sister-in-law and her mother-in-law, Naomi. The three women were widows with no protection, only liabilities. So Ruth, still young and strong enough to work in the fields, insisted on accompanying Naomi back to her original home in Bethlehem.

Once there, Ruth worked daily, harvesting barley, and later wheat, in the fields of Naomi's relative, Boaz, a prominent man in town. Often, the Ruth/Boaz story is told like an American love story, complete with buff man and beautiful maiden. But Boaz was probably an old married guy, maybe missing some teeth, perhaps walking with a cane.

Ruth could have found a handsome young man. After all, she was probably only about twenty-five years old. But that would have meant

---

[8] Paul Bender, *J Vibrations ezine,* Issue 8 [online] <www.jvibe.com/jvibrations/issue8/responsa2.shtml>.

leaving Naomi to fend for herself with no one responsible to care for her. No young husband would want to care for the former husband's mother. But if Ruth married one of Naomi's near relatives, the relative would be obligated to feed Ruth's mother-in-law, too.

The fact that Naomi stayed home while Ruth gleaned suggests Naomi may have been in poor health. And she certainly had a whiny attitude! Imagine you were Ruth, having left everything you'd ever known to care for Naomi. And as your mother-in-law stands next to you greeting her friends upon her return, she tells everyone, "I've come back empty." Wouldn't you want to ask, "Hello? Don't I count for something?"

Before long, Boaz noticed what a great person Ruth was. So he instructed his servants to help her. When word got back to Naomi about it, she sent Ruth to propose marriage to Boaz, a man who, as mentioned, was much older. Boaz was even more amazed by the young woman's willingness to marry him than he was by her self-lessness in accompanying Naomi to her homeland. So he married Ruth.

Now think about this—Ruth was "infertile" for a decade in a culture that offered children as human sacrifices. Then, she lost her husband and any means of security. Being childless was particularly difficult in a day in which children were the parents' only Meals-on-Wheels and retirement programs. Losing all hope of security must have devastated her. Yet even in her pain, she still placed someone else's needs above her own.

Then, after all those losses, when a happy ending looked impossible, Ruth went on to have a child and, as ancestress to Jesus, a name that would last forever.

When God allows suffering, it's to bring about something better in the long run. His plans are always good and always just. Unlike us, the Almighty Sovereign One can see the big picture, can take the long view. Will you trust God with your present, and your future?

Prayer: Heavenly Father, thank You for Your faithfulness in keeping Your promises. Thank You that at a time when Your people were sinking deeply into sin, You were blessing them in ways they could not even imagine. Thank You for taking a lost young woman with no pedigree and raising her up to the company of the eternally blessed. Help me, like her, to show loyal love even to those who don't appreciate my sacrifices on their behalf. And help me to trust Your heart—that Your plans are always right, Your ways are always just—even when I can't see in the dark. In the name of Ruth's descendant, and Your Son, Jesus Christ, Amen.

For Memorization: The women of the village said, "Can this be Naomi?" But she replied to them, "Don't call me 'Naomi'! Call me 'Mara' because the Sovereign One has treated me very harshly. I left here full, but the Lord has caused me to return empty-handed. Why do you call me 'Naomi,' seeing that the Lord has opposed me, and the Sovereign One has caused me to suffer?" (Ruth 1:19–21).

WEEK 2 OF 4

Running on Empty: Ruth 1

Ruth 1:22—"So Naomi returned, accompanied by her Moabite daughter-in-law Ruth, who came back with her from the region of Moab. (Now they arrived in Bethlehem at the beginning of the barley harvest.)"

My husband and I endured a decade of infertility that included seven early pregnancy losses and three failed adoptions before the successful adoption of our daughter. Several months after one of the adoptions fell through, I joined a ministry team going to Mexico over Mother's Day weekend. When I realized I'd miss the Hallmark holiday in the U.S., I rejoiced. Little did I realize Mother's Day in Mexico, which fell the Wednesday we were there, is an even bigger deal.

By Wednesday night, I wanted to fly home. On the eve of the big day, the men arrived at midnight to serenade the moms. On Wednesday everyone stayed home to observe the national holiday. And that night, members of our "sister church," threw a big party. I couldn't escape it! I hated to take anyone else's joy away or cry at their party, but I just couldn't bring myself to celebrate with them. My grief was too raw.

After the fiesta, we had a church service. Our pastor, who is fluent in Spanish, delivered the message. In his sermon, he pointed out that the holiday is hard for lots of people: those who've lost mothers; those who've lost children; those who can't be mothers, for whatever reason; and those who are estranged from their mothers or children. Then, he challenged every woman present to leave a spiritual legacy. I sat there weeping, wondering if the pain would ever end, yet asking God to help me think beyond my temporary angst.

At the end of the service, the men presented each woman with a carnation—just one. Yet, a guy on my team, a man who, with his wife, had lost a baby at term, walked over to me, burst into tears, and shoved a bouquet of carnations into my palm.

Several years later, my husband and I returned to that little church with a daughter in our arms. Many of the same team members accompanied us, and we all rejoiced as we entered the place where I'd worshipped with open wounds. This time, however, I had a child.

During a worship service on that trip, a vocalist sang, "God Will Make a Way" And then something profound happened. My pastor, who had watched me weep through his entire Mother's Day sermon years before, made eye contact. Then, he quietly rose from his seat, and went to sit in exactly the same spot where I'd been when he delivered his message. He looked at me and smiled.

My vision blurred, but this time the tears fogging my eyes were joyous. Without a word, my brother in Christ used a place to communicate something powerful about God.

In the grand scheme of redemption history, God uses Bethlehem as a place to communicate something important. Originally called Ephrath (Gen. 35:16, 19; 48:7; Ruth 4:11), the "house of bread" was also called Beth-lehem Ephratah (Micah 5:2), and Beth-lehem-judah (1 Sam. 17:12). Later it was called "the city of David" (Luke 2:4). The first big event recorded there was the burial of Rachel nearby, after she died birthing Benjamin (Gen. 48:7). The next we hear of Bethlehem, it's in that gnarly section about the gang rape at the end of Judges, which we read about last week. After that, a man name Elimilech leaves Bethlehem because of famine. So Bethlehem's history is one of sadness, of loss, of sin, of need.

Yet "God will make a way when there seems to be no way." A childless girl from Moab goes on to find in "the house of bread" the sustenance, both physical and spiritual, that she and her mother-in-law need. Her new town five miles south of Jerusalem in Judea's hill country lies at an altitude of about 2,500 feet. And that means she can see the land of Moab, visible to the southeast, from her new home. From this lofty height, she can remember: "My arms were empty, but now they're full."

What she doesn't even know at the time is that her child will be the ancestor of David, Israel's second king. Saul anointed David in Bethlehem, and from its well three heroes risked their lives to bring water to their king (2 Sam. 23:13-17). Then came Micah's big prediction that the little city would be the birthplace of "Him whose goings forth have been of old" (Micah 5:2, KJV).

You know the rest of the "little town's" story. The angels appeared and announced good news to trembling shepherds: "Unto you is born this day in the city of David a Savior, which is Christ the Lord."

Sometimes the place can say more than the words.

Where was Peter standing when he denied the Lord three times? By a fire (Luke 22:56). Where was Jesus standing when he gave Peter three chances to declare his love? By a fire. (John 21:9ff).

One year, my husband and I accompanied a medical team to Russia, and our group met in a place where KGB agents used to meet. Only this time we held an Easter service there.

What are your places of loss and failure and pain? Ask God to make a way. The Lord can do it, even when there seems to be no way. With God all things are possible (Matt. 19:26).

MONDAY: THE HOUSE OF BREAD

1. Pray for insight from the Holy Spirit. Then read chapter 1 of the Book of Ruth:

1:1 During the time of the judges there was a famine in the land of Judah. So a man from Bethlehem in Judah went to live as a resident foreigner in the region of Moab, along with his wife and two sons. **1:2** (Now the man's name was Elimelech, his wife was Naomi, and his two sons were Mahlon and Kilion. They were of the clan of Ephrath from Bethlehem in Judah.) They entered the region of Moab and settled there. **1:3** Sometime later Naomi's husband Elimelech died, so she and her two sons were left alone. **1:4** So her sons married Moabite women. (One was named Orpah and the other Ruth.) And they continued to live there about ten years. **1:5** Then Naomi's two sons, Mahlon and Kilion, also died. So the woman was left all alone—bereaved of her two children as well as her husband! **1:6** So she decided to return home from the region of Moab, accompanied by her daughters-in-law, because while she was living in Moab she had heard that the LORD had shown concern for his people, reversing the famine by providing abundant crops.

1:7 Now as she and her two daughters-in-law began to leave the place where she had been living to return to the land of Judah, **1:8** Naomi said to her two daughters-in-law, "Listen to me! Each of you should return to your mother's home! May the LORD show you the same kind of devotion that you have shown to your deceased husbands and to me! 1:9 May the LORD enable each of you to find security in the home of a new husband!" Then she kissed them goodbye and they wept loudly. **1:10** But they said to her, "No! We will return with you to your people."

1:11 But Naomi replied, "Go back home, my daughters! There is no reason for you to return to Judah with me! I am no longer capable of giving birth to sons who might become your husbands! **1:12** Go back home, my daughters! For I am too old to get married again. Even if I thought that there was hope that I could get married tonight and conceive sons, **1:13** surely you would not want to wait until they were old enough to marry! Surely you would not remain unmarried all that time! No, my daughters, you must not return with me. For my intense suffering is too much for you to bear. For the LORD is afflicting me!"

1:14 Again they wept loudly. Then Orpah kissed her mother-in-law goodbye, but Ruth clung tightly to her. **1:15** So Naomi said, "Look, your sister-in-law is returning to her people and to her god. Follow your sister-in-law back home!" **1:16** But Ruth replied,

"Stop urging me to abandon you!

For wherever you go, I will go.

Wherever you live, I will live.

Your people will become my people,

and your God will become my God.

1:17 Wherever you die, I will die—and there I will be buried.

May the LORD punish me severely if I do not keep my promise!

Only death will be able to separate me from you!"

1:18 When Naomi realized that Ruth was determined to go

with her, she stopped trying to dissuade her. **1:19** So the two of them journeyed together until they arrived in Bethlehem.

When they entered Bethlehem, the whole village was excited about their arrival. The women of the village said, "Can this be Naomi?" **1:20** But she replied to them, "Don't call me 'Naomi'! Call me 'Mara' because the Sovereign One has treated me very harshly. **1:21** I left here full, but the LORD has caused me to return empty-handed. Why do you call me 'Naomi', seeing that the LORD has opposed me, and the Sovereign One has caused me to suffer?" **1:22** So Naomi returned, accompanied by her Moabite daughter-in-law Ruth, who came back with her from the region of Moab. (Now they arrived in Bethlehem at the beginning of the barley harvest.)

Go back and circle every reference to "Bethlehem" or "place."
Draw a box around every form of the word "Moab."
Underline every reference associated with food, such as famine, crops, and harvest.

What contrasts did you find in Ruth 1 (examples: the difference in the two girls' responses; the contrast in Naomi's two names)?

_____

_____

_____

If you were to give yourself a name that describes your current circumstances, what would it be?

_____

_____

_____

What names for God did you see in Ruth 1?

_____

_____

TUESDAY: FAMINE AND FEAST

1. Pray for insight from the Holy Spirit. Then read Ruth 1:1–6.

> **1:1** During the time of the judges there was a famine in the land of Judah. So a man from Bethlehem in Judah went to live as a resident foreigner in the region of Moab, along with his wife and two sons. **1:2** (Now the man's name was Elimelech, his wife was Naomi, and his two sons were Mahlon and Kilion. They were of the clan of Ephrath from Bethlehem in Judah.) They entered the region of Moab and settled there. **1:3** Sometime later Naomi's husband Elimelech died, so she and her two sons were left alone. **1:4** So her sons married Moabite women. (One was named Orpah and the other Ruth.) And they continued to live there about ten years. **1:5** Then Naomi's two sons, Mahlon and Kilion, also died. So the woman was left all alone—bereaved of her two children as well as her husband! **1:6** So she decided to return home from the region of Moab, accompanied by her daughters-in-law, because while she was living in Moab she had heard that the LORD had shown concern for his people, reversing the famine by providing abundant crops.

Today 15 million children die of hunger every year. The World Health Organization estimates that one-third of the world is well-fed; one-third is under-fed; one-third is starving. While you read this page, at least two hundred people will have died of starvation. And over four million will die this year.[1]

What is the longest you've ever gone without food? Why?

_____

_____

_____

[1] "The World Hunger Problem: Facts, Figures and Statistics," Thinkquest web site, Oracle Education Foundation, http://library.thinkquest.org/C002291/high/present/stats.htm, accessed January 3, 2007.

How did you feel?

_____

_____

How might a hungry stomach influence your thoughts about God?

_____

_____

3. *Famine in the land of Judah* (1:1)—Barrenness, of crops, animals, and people, is a motif we see in the Old Testament. Sometimes it's linked to God's curse. The Book of Deuteronomy, which is the record of the Law as God gave it to Moses, is actually laid out in the language and structure of an ancient contract. This contract is between God and Israel like that of a suzerain lord and his vassal subjects. Consider the health of Naomi's two sons in light of the following section of the "contract":

> If you are not careful to observe all the words of this law which are written in this book, to fear this honored and awesome name, the LORD your God, then the LORD will bring extraordinary plagues on you and your descendants, even severe and lasting plagues, and miserable and chronic sicknesses ... Every sickness and every plague which, not written in the book of this law, the LORD will bring on you until you are destroyed. Then you shall be left few in number, whereas you were as the stars of heaven for multitude, because you did not obey the LORD your God... and you shall be torn from the land where you are entering to possess it. . . . And among those nations you shall find no rest, and there shall be no resting place for the sole of your foot; but there the LORD will give you a trembling heart, failing of eyes, and despair of soul. (Deut. 28:58–65 NASB)

It's important to understand that the law was like a treaty between God and His nation. That said, if we see hungry people today, we should not assume their difficulty is due to God's punishment. Or when an epidemic hits, we should not conclude that the sick are out of God's will. The message of Job is that there's not always a clear cause/effect relationship between individual sin and suffering. We're talking here about blessing and cursing on a national level within a specific contract. In the context of the Book of Ruth, the whole landscape of Bethlehem was so devoid of food that its citizens were scattered.

It's important to note that God gave the list of "blessings and cursings" to a nation under the Law, which the New Testament describes as the "old covenant." Anyone who has trusted Christ for salvation lives under a different, a new, covenant (Heb. 9:15). Today the primary focus of God's covenants has shifted from the nation of Israel as a group to individuals (who make up the universal church) in whom the Spirit dwells. And the focus has shifted from visible to spiritual realities. While the events in the "first testament" provide helpful instruction (1 Cor. 10:11), when we wrongly assume the same "system" is in operation today, we grossly distort the truth.

With these things in mind, consider that the famine in Bethlehem was so great as to force descendants of Abraham to seek refuge in enemy territory. They went to Moab, of all places! Then two of the three men were sickly, and all died. What do you think the author of the Book of Ruth wants us to wonder about the spiritual health of the nation under such conditions?

---

4. *Return home* (1:6). Naomi and Ruth's trip required a journey of about fifty miles through rough terrain, both mountainous as well as barren area around the Dead Sea. Imagine two poor women on foot embarking on this difficult fifty-mile hike.

The longest hike I've ever taken was to the bottom of the Grand Canyon and back with a twenty-pound pack on my back. (It's thirteen miles down, shorter—but steeper—on the way back.) My husband and dad had to help me carry it part of the way. I kept myself going at the end by chanting "Hot. Shower. Hot. Shower." I alternated that chant with, "The things you do for love. The things you do for love." What's the longest trek you've ever made? What do you think it would be like to walk fifty miles carrying everything you owned?

_____

_____

_____

5. *From the region of Moab* (1:6). Last week we read about Israelite/Moabite relations. Ruth's label as a "Moabitess" was a stigma. One of my friends used to describe her fifty-year old daughter as "my adopted daughter." I got the distinct impression every time she said it that she was trying to distance herself from her girl. (I'm glad my other friends didn't describe their grown children with modifiers like "my contraceptive—failure son.") And I would hate for my niece and nephew to describe me as their "white aunt." (They're African-American.) The story of Ruth reveals that the girl referred to as a "Moabitess" (with noses upturned) acted more righteously than those who should have been a testimony to her.

Why was it a stigma to be from Moab? It's important to know who the Moabites were. As we saw last week, after the destruction of Sodom and Gomorrah, Lot's two surviving daughters feared they would never marry and have children. So they got their father drunk and slept with him. Both conceived, and they named their children Moab and Ben-Ammi (Gen. 19:30–38). Apparently these women could see God preserve them through a global flood, but they couldn't trust Him for offspring! Moab and Ben-Ammi, the children of incest, later became the patriarchs of the Moabites and Ammonites, two nations that warred frequently with Israel.

The Moabites worshipped Chemosh, a despicable deity requiring child sacrifice. They also worshiped Baals and Ashtoreths, fertility deities. These false gods were a snare to the Israelites during the period of the judges. Consider this description in Judges 10:6: "Again the Israelites did evil in the eyes of the LORD. They served the Baals and the Ashtoreths, and the gods of Aram, the gods of Sidon, the gods of Moab, the gods of the Ammonites and the gods of the Philistines."

When Moses received the Law, the instructions about the Ammonites and Moabites were clear: "An Ammonite or Moabite may not enter the assembly of the Lord; to the tenth generation none of their descendants shall ever do so, for they did not meet you with food and water on the way as you came from Egypt, and furthermore, they hired Balaam son of Beor of Pethor in Aram Naharaim to curse you.

But the Lord your God refused to listen to Balaam and changed the curse to a blessing, for the Lord your God loves you. You must not seek peace and prosperity for them through all the ages to come" (Deut. 23:3–6).

What does it say to you about God that he chose a Moabitess as one of the five women in the genealogy of Jesus?

_____

_____

_____

6. *For* [Naomi] *heard in the land of Moab that the LORD had considered His people and given them food* (1:6). We could understand the word "that" two ways. Either, "The reason God visited His people was to give them food" or "The way in which God visited His people was by giving them food." I suspect it's the latter. The reason I used the verb "visited" rather than "considered" is because the Hebrew word is translated in other places as "tending to" or "visiting." (It's a little awkward to translate it that way into English, since we don't equate "visit" with "look after" or "tend.") But I like the word "visited" because it says God did more than think about these people in their need. The Lord showed up.

Happy days returned to Israel and apparently word reached Naomi in Moab, some fifty miles away. The Hebrew word behind "LORD" in verse 6 is "Yahweh," the Self-existing One. When you see "LORD" in all-capital letters, Yahweh is the name for God that appears in the underlying text. It means "to generation of generation" or "I am that I am" or even more likely, "I will be that I will be." When Jesus says, "Before Abraham was born 'I Am,' " (John 8:58), the people picked up stones to kill him. Basically, Jesus claimed to be this same Self-Existing One. What does the very name of God say about the character and nature of the Almighty?

_____

_____

_____

7. When Israel was in need, God visited His people to give them food. In his Sermon on the Mount, our Lord taught his disciples to pray "Give us this day our daily bread" (Matt. 6:11). The need for daily bread is real and urgent for most of the world's inhabitants. Spend a few moments acknowledging God as the source of your abundant provision. List ways God has provided for you.

_____

_____

_____

8. Considering the worldwide need for daily bread, what and with whom can you share the resources God has given you?

_____

_____

_____

9. Jesus said we can't live by bread alone, but "by every word that comes from the mouth of God." How, and with whom, can you share God's "every word"?

_____

_____

_____

WEDNESDAY: EXTREME DEVOTION

1. Ask the Holy Spirit to lead you as you interact with God's truth. Then, read Ruth 1:7–13:

> **1:7** Now as she and her two daughters-in-law began to leave the place where she had been living to return to the land of Judah,

1:8 Naomi said to her two daughters-in-law, "Listen to me! Each of you should return to your mother's home! May the LORD show you the same kind of **devotion** that you have shown to your deceased husbands and to me! **1:9** May the LORD enable each of you to find security in the home of a new husband!" Then she kissed them goodbye and they wept loudly. **1:10** But they said to her, "No! We will return with you to your people."

1:11 But Naomi replied, "Go back home, my daughters! There is no reason for you to return to Judah with me! I am no longer capable of giving birth to sons who might become your husbands! **1:12** Go back home, my daughters! For I am too old to get married again. Even if I thought that there was hope that I could get married tonight and conceive sons, **1:13** surely you would not want to wait until they were old enough to marry! Surely you would not remain unmarried all that time! No, my daughters, you must not return with me. For my intense suffering is too much for you to bear. For the LORD is afflicting me!"

The same devotion. In Ruth 1:8, Naomi tells her daughters-in-law, "May the LORD show you the same kind of devotion that you have shown to your deceased husbands and to me!" The word for "devotion" is *hesed*. (It's pronounced with a hard "h" and rhymes with the two-syllable form of "blesséd.") It's an important word throughout the Old Testament. In fact, if you're going to memorize one Hebrew word in addition to "shalom" and "Hallelujah," it should probably be *hesed*. Why? Because God uses it to describe his own character (Ex. 34:6). In fact, *hesed* seems to be the one word chosen above all others to summarize what God is like: full of loyal, committed, merciful, enduring, faithful, covenant-keeping love. An act of *hesed* is often demonstrated as assistance shown to a more vulnerable party, to one unable to help him or herself.

That loyal, faithful, covenant-keeping love, hesed, is a key theme in the Book of Ruth:

> **Ruth 1:8** "Naomi said to her two daughters-in-law, 'Listen to me! Each of you should return to your mother's home! May the LORD show you the same kind of **devotion** that you have shown to your deceased husbands and to me!' "

> **Ruth 2:20** Naomi said to her daughter-in-law, "May [Boaz] be rewarded by the Lord because he has shown **loyalty** to the living on behalf of the dead!" Then Naomi said to her, "This man is a close relative of ours; he is our guardian."

Ruth 3:10 [Boaz] said [to Ruth], "May you be rewarded by the Lord, my dear! This act of devotion is greater than what you did before. For you have not sought to marry one of the young men, whether rich or poor.

In the past, translators have often rendered hesed as "lovingkindness." Yet we use the word "love" in English for anything from "I love raspberries," to "I love my husband." We're not talking about the same quality or depth of love! My love for raspberries requires no sacrifice; my love for my husband sometimes does. *Hesed* is not an emotional love or an attitude as much as it is an expression of deep faithfulness and loyalty.

Humans are notorious for letting their "yes" mean "no," for making empty promises, breaking vows, failing to follow through. From Peter's "I will not deny you," to the elder Bush's "Read my lips: no new taxes," human commitments and good intentions often fail to last. Even the most godly husband and wife, when reciting their wedding vows, add, "Till death do us part." At best, their loyalty lasts some seventy years. Only God alone can say, "I will never leave you or forsake you."

2. How has God shown *hesed* to you?

_____

_____

_____

3. What human(s) has shown you *hesed*? How?

_____

_____

_____

4. To whom have you shown *hesed*? How?

_____

_____

_____

5. To whom can you demonstrate *hesed* this week? What will you do?

_____

_____

_____

6. We've considered levirate law—the Old Testament practice of impregnating a childless sister-in-law if one's brother died. The practice guaranteed to the deceased that he be remembered at a time when no one had camcorders or photo albums or picture frames. And it kept one family's land from going to another's. More importantly, it provided a place and provision for the otherwise vulnerable widow. The practice may seem strange to us in that what was to them an act of *hesed* might look a little like unfaithfulness today. At this point I'm reminded of what a theologian friend teaches: "All scripture is redemptive, but it may not be redemptive to you." To Naomi, at the time, the law would have been a wonderful help if she'd had a living son. As mentioned, Naomi had in mind the levirate law when she urged her daughters-in-law to return rather than go with her:

> **1:11** But Naomi replied, "Go back home, my daughters! There is no reason for you to return to Judah with me! I am no longer capable of giving birth to sons who might become your husbands! **1:12** Go back home, my daughters! For I am too old to get married again. Even if I thought that there was hope that I could get married tonight and conceive sons, **1:13** surely you would not want to wait until they were old enough to marry! Surely you would not remain unmarried all that time! No, my daughters, you must not return with me.

Understanding how levirate law worked is essential to understanding the Book of Ruth. During Jesus' ministry, the Sadducees tried to trip him up with a question about levirate law. Mark's Gospel records the interaction (Mark 12:18–25):

> Sadducees (who say there is no resurrection) also came to him and asked him, "Teacher, Moses wrote for us: 'If a man's brother dies and leaves a wife but no children, that man must marry the widow and father children for his brother." There were seven brothers. The first one married, and when he died he had no children. The second married her and died without any children, and likewise the third.

None of the seven had children. Finally, the woman died too. In the resurrection, when they rise again, whose wife will she be? For all seven had married her." Jesus said to them, "Aren't you deceived for this reason, because you don't know the scriptures or the power of God? For when they rise from the dead, they neither marry nor are given in marriage, but are like angels in heaven."

Consider how levirate law played out in the life of Tamar back in the early days of the nation of Israel's history. Tamar was the daughter-in-law of Judah. Remember him? If you recall the story of Joseph and his coat of many colors, you remember Judah as one of the brothers who sold Joseph into slavery. As one of the twelve sons of Jacob ("Israel"), Judah had a lineage that was essential to the Jewish nation.

Genesis 38:6 Judah acquired a wife for Er his firstborn; her name was Tamar. **38:7** But Er, Judah's firstborn, was evil in the Lord's sight, so the Lord killed him.

38:8 Then Judah said to Onan, "Have sexual relations with your brother's wife and fulfill the duty of a brother-in-law to her so that you may raise up a descendant for your brother." **38:9** But Onan knew that the child would not be considered his. So whenever he had sexual relations with his brother's wife, he withdrew prematurely so as not to give his brother a descendant. **38:10** What he did was evil in the Lord's sight, so the Lord killed him too.

38:11 Then Judah said to his daughter-in-law Tamar, "Live as a widow in your father's house until Shelah my son grows up." For he thought, "I don't want him to die like his brothers." So Tamar went and lived in her father's house.

38:12 After some time Judah's wife, the daughter of Shua, died. After Judah was consoled, he left for Timnah to visit his sheepshearers, along with his friend Hirah the Adullamite. **38:13** Tamar was told, "Look, your father-in-law is going up to Timnah to shear his sheep." **38:14** So she removed her widow's clothes and covered herself with a veil. She wrapped herself and sat at the entrance to Enaim which is on the way to Timnah. (She did this because she saw that she had not been given to Shelah as a wife, even though he had now grown up.)

38:15 When Judah saw her, he thought she was a prostitute because she had covered her face. **38:16** He turned aside to her along the road and said, "Come on! I want to have sex with you." (He did not realize it was his daughter-in-law.) She asked, "What will you give me in exchange for having sex with you?" **38:17** He replied, "I'll send you a young goat from the flock." She asked, "Will you give me a pledge until you send it?" **38:18** He said, "What pledge should I give you?" She replied, "Your seal, your cord, and the staff that's in your hand." So he gave them to her and had sex with her. She became pregnant by him. **38:19** She left immediately, removed her veil, and put on her widow's clothes.

38:20 Then Judah had his friend Hirah the Adullamite take a young goat to get back from the woman the items he had given in pledge, but Hirah could not find her. **38:21** He asked the men who were there, "Where is the cult prostitute who was at Enaim by the road?" But they replied, "There has been no cult prostitute here." **38:22** So he returned to Judah and said, "I couldn't find her. Moreover, the men of the place said, 'There has been no cult prostitute here.'" **38:23** Judah said, "Let her keep the things for herself. Otherwise we will appear to be dishonest. I did indeed send this young goat, but you couldn't find her."

38:24 After three months Judah was told, "Your daughter-in-law Tamar has turned to prostitution, and as a result she has become pregnant." Judah said, "Bring her out and let her be burned!" **38:25** While they were bringing her out, she sent word to her father-in-law: "I am pregnant by the man to whom these belong." Then she said, "Identify the one to whom the seal, cord, and staff belong." **38:26** Judah recognized them and said, "She is more upright than I am, because I wouldn't give her to Shelah my son." He did not have sexual relations with her again.

38:27 When it was time for her to give birth, there were twins in her womb. **38:28** While she was giving birth, one child put out his hand, and the midwife took a scarlet thread and tied it on his hand, saying, "This one came out first." **38:29** But then he drew back his hand, and his brother came out before him. She said, "How you have broken out of the womb!" So he was named Perez. **38:30** Afterward his brother came out—the one who had the scarlet thread on his hand—and he was named Zerah.

Perhaps it would help to know a few details about this narrative. First, Onan's story has been used by some in the church through the centuries to argue against masturbation and contraception. They would've been wise to seek other "proof" texts. God's judgment of Onan had nothing to do with those things. It had to do with his failure to show *hesed* to his deceased brother. Onan was willing to degrade his brother's wife by using and discarding her, but he was unwilling to take the economic risk of impregnating her. (By the way, "early withdrawal," or *coitus interruptus,* is sometimes called "Onanism." How's that for a legacy?)

Often if a brother was unavailable, a father-in-law stepped in to guarantee his son's legacy. In her book, *Lost Women of the Bible,* Carolyn Custis James explains, "Investigators of ancient history have uncovered ancient Hittite and Assyrian laws that regulated the levirate duty. These documents not only placed responsibility on the brother of the deceased but, interestingly enough, they also supported marriage of the father-in-law to his son's widow if no brother fulfilled this duty. Although biblical regulations later prohibit this, it seems plausible, especially in light of Tamar's conduct, that in Judah's day the father-in-law was responsible if his son failed to fulfill his duty. According to such laws, and also to the Bible's view of Tamar, conception by a father-in-law was a legitimate means of saving a family member from being cut off. Furthermore, now that Judah was a widow, no wrong would be done against his wife."[2]

For this reason, we should most likely interpret Tamar's seduction of her father-in-law as an act of *hesed* toward her deceased husband, evil as he was, rather than as the act of a flagrantly immoral woman. Judah was immoral in having relations with an unknown prostitute. Tamar was moral in seeking a levirate union to leave a legacy for her wicked husband. Consider how far she was willing to go to give him a continuing name. Genesis 38:26 and Ruth 4:12 both serve as evidence testifying that what we're to interpret Tamar's actions as righteous.

6. What do you think it must have been like to be Tamar, first married to an evil man, and then abused by his brother, then lied to by his immoral father?

---

[2] Carolyn Custis-James. *Lost Women of the Bible.* Grand Rapids, Michigan: Zondervan, 2005, p. 111. The chapter on Tamar is well-researched and brilliantly argued.

7. Would you say Tamar went beyond the call of duty? Why or why not?

_____

_____

_____

_____

8. Who is an example to you of extreme devotion?

_____

_____

_____

_____

There is no reason for you to return to Judah with me! (1:11). Can you imagine? Naomi felt more broke than an Enron retiree. The phrasing suggests Naomi is actually asking this as a rhetorical question: "Why should you go with me?" In other words, "Give me one good reason why you should feel obligated." Clearly the levirate law couldn't come into play, and Naomi had nothing to offer her daughters-in-law. What benefit, then, did they have in leaving their homeland and going with a penniless widow?

"For my intense suffering is too much for you to bear" (1:13)— The phrasing here could also be translated, "[My suffering] is harder for me than for you." Such a rendering seems to fit Naomi's character. It's like saying, "Get out while you can. I'm a cursed woman." Both the NIV and NASB translators understand it this way.

Another possibility is the idea that "life is harder for me on account of you," rendered by the KJV translators as, "It grieveth me much for your sakes." That is, her daughter-in-law's losses have only added to Naomi's losses. In addition to her own grief, she sees them suffer, and they'd continue to suffer by not having husbands if they came with her. She's not necessarily blaming them for her bitterness.

9. Naomi said, "The Lord is afflicting me!" (1:13)

A. Was the Lord truly afflicting her?

_____

_____

_____

B. Do you see a difference between "God is afflicting me" and "God has allowed my affliction"? Is it worth making a distinction?

_____

_____

_____

10. What do you think of Naomi's view of God? Through what spiritual grid would you view your circumstances if you lost your entire family of a husband and two sons? What do you think is an appropriate spiritual response to such a situation?

_____

_____

_____

11. Knowing how the story turns out, what do you think God was doing in and through Naomi in the long term? Do you think she was being punished? Why or why not?

_____

_____

_____

12. Based on what you know of the story, what can we learn about how to view God's involvement in our circumstances?

_____

_____

_____

THURSDAY: YOUR GOD, MY GOD

1. Ask the Holy Spirit to lead you as you interact with God's truth. Then, read Ruth 1:14–19.

> **1:14** Again they wept loudly. Then Orpah kissed her mother-in-law goodbye, but Ruth clung tightly to her. **1:15** So Naomi said, "Look, your sister-in-law is returning to her people and to her god. Follow your sister-in-law back home!" **1:16** But Ruth replied,
>
> "Stop urging me to abandon you!
>
> For wherever you go, I will go.
>
> Wherever you live, I will live.
>
> Your people will become my people,
>
> and your God will become my God.
>
> **1:17** Wherever you die, I will die—and there I will be buried.
>
> May the LORD punish me severely if I do not keep my promise!
>
> Only death will be able to separate me from you!"
>
> **1:18** When Naomi realized that Ruth was determined to go with her, she stopped trying to dissuade her. **1:19** So the two of them journeyed together until they arrived in Bethlehem.

Orpah gets a bad rap. She was not wrong to return home. She had stayed with her mother-in-law after the death of all the husbands, and she was even starting out to go with Naomi. It was Naomi's logical argument that dissuaded Orpah from going to Bethlehem. If we think of Orpah as doing the wrong thing, and we think of Ruth as doing the right thing, we miss a key point in the story. Orpah did what was expected. She fulfilled her obligation. She did what anybody would logically do. Yet Ruth showed excessive, far-beyond-what-was-expected devotion both to her mother-in-law and to her dead husband. She showed extreme *hesed*. Remember how we saw that acts of *hesed* are often done on behalf of a more vulnerable party? Naomi was the vulnerable one here, even though Ruth herself was also extremely vulnerable. Ruth was able to help Naomi in a way that Naomi could not help herself.

The friend of a friend received divorce papers from his wife. She proceeded to sue not only for half of the estate, but for heirloom possessions her husband had brought with him into the marriage. He told her, "Take anything and everything. I'm not going to fight you. It's just material stuff, and I don't want a battle in court. Just, please, don't take from me the ability to build a new life by suing me against money I don't have and can't earn." In the end, he gave her far more than the law would have let her take. And they ended up back together again. What got her attention? "Nobody else loves like that!"

Think of people in your life who need help.

What is expected/required/right to do, difficult as it may be?

_____

_____

_____

What would go beyond required to generous?

_____

_____

_____

_____

Beyond that, what would be an astonishingly, unheard-of kind thing to do?

_____

_____

_____

_____

3. Pray about your response. Is there someone who needs you to show
hesed? Someone who is vulnerable and cannot help him or herself?
Someone for whom you need to go far beyond what's required?

_____

_____

_____

_____

• *But Ruth clung tightly to her* (1:14). In its verb form, "cling"
involves sticking to, attaching one's self, holding fast to. In its noun
form, it's used in association with soldering. "Cling" here seems to
suggest more than Ruth's physically wrapping her arms around
Naomi's neck, though it certainly could have involved that. Ruth also
appears to be attaching herself to and associating with Naomi in the
sense of being joined to her for more than this moment. She's going
to follow Naomi. The context that follows bears this out.

• *To her god* (1:15). The text tells us that Orpah returned to her
people and to her god. The word for "god" is "elohim." Elohim is
one of the names of our God. The "im" ending in Hebrew can be
used as a plural (gods); as a suffix for "mega" (our God is a mega-
God!); or to indicate intensity (the main god of a territory). Whether
the text means Elohim, our God, or elohim, a false god or gods, only
the context tells.

So why does it say here that Orpah returned to her god rather
than her gods? "Elohim" is used in other places (such as Judges 11:24;
1 Kings 11:33) where a certain god of a region is referred to. So this
time the "im" ending is probably to suggest intensity rather than plu-
rality. While Moab was polytheistic, Chemosh was the national god of
Moab, so most translators prefer the singular.

• *Your God will become my God* (1:16). Ruth says, "Your elohim
[will become] my Elohim." Sometimes we hear Ruth's beautiful
words of faithfulness cited in wedding ceremonies. Some of my friends

think the words are ripped horribly out of context, and in one sense they're right. Ruth was not marrying Naomi and it was not romantic love she had in mind! On the other hand, why not quote from an extreme example of *hesed* in the context of two people promising to stay faithful to each other and love sacrificially until death parts them?

_____

_____

_____

4. Earlier in the chapter, Naomi is determined to return home because she has heard that the LORD has "visited" his people. God graciously provides for the physical needs of the nation, and she acknowledges the spiritual provision. Then Ruth embraces Naomi's Elohim. Naomi clearly was not an evangelist. She didn't tell Orpah, "Come to Bethlehem with me so you can worship the true God!" Yet, Naomi attributed improving circumstances to God's sovereignty. Make a list of places where you see God's sovereignty at work in your own life.

_____

_____

_____

_____

_____

5. Ruth had a "non-traditional" conversion, to say the least! In the process of showing compassion to someone else, she decided to embrace that person's God. Have you embraced Elohim as the one true God? If so, what circumstances led to your conversion? If not, why not?

_____

_____

_____

_____

6. Spend some time giving thanks to God for having a trustworthy sovereign hand that's at work in your life.

_____

_____

_____

_____

May the LORD punish me severely if I do not keep my promise! Only death will be able to separate me from you! (1:17)—Significantly, this may be the first time Ruth has ever uttered the name of Yahweh. It's the only time in the book she says "Yahweh," though the townspeople and Naomi frequently use this name for God. Ruth's use of the divine name here makes her statement all the more dramatic.

We have to fill in some blanks to get a smooth translation, though. A more literal (though rougher) rendering would be, "Thus may Yahweh do to me, and even more—only death will separate you from me." If a parent tells a child, "Clean your room, or else. . .," the child does not have to know what the "or else" will be, nor does the parent have to figure out the penalty on the spot for the threat to be real. It's not a complete sentence, but no one corrects the "grammar."

Ruth's incomplete sentence suggests something much more horrible than any penalty a parent might impose in such a situation. In her day, when a curse was too awful to speak, it was left to the listener to fill in the blanks. So she's saying, "We will not be separated until death parts us—or else!" Picture her drawing her index finger across her throat or some similar dramatic gesture, and you get the idea.

We see a similar grammatical structure in 1 Sam. 14:44, where Saul said, "God do so to me and more also; you shall surely die, Jonathan!" It's an oath with the absence of statement about what the curse will be, followed by a prediction of what will happen.

In 2 Samuel 3:9, we read, "So may God do to Abner and more! For just what the LORD has sworn to David, that will I accomplish for him." Again, we see an oath with the absence of statement about what the curse will be, followed by a prediction of what will happen.

We find twelve such uses of this formula in the Old Testament, and the calamity that the speaker predicts is never named. So we know Ruth is invoking the same kind of oath and is swearing that some horrible death would have to befall her before she'd separate herself from Naomi. Imagine Naomi's expression: "Well, if you put it that way!" Notice how it stops her argument (Ruth 1:18).

Friday: Bitter, Not Sweet

1. Ask the Holy Spirit to lead you as you interact with God's truth. Then read Ruth 1:20–22.

> **1:20** But she replied to them, "Don't call me 'Naomi'! Call me 'Mara' because the Sovereign One has treated me very harshly. **1:21** I left here full, but the LORD has caused me to return empty-handed. Why do you call me 'Naomi', seeing that the LORD has opposed me, and the Sovereign One has caused me to suffer?" **1:22** So Naomi returned, accompanied by her Moabite daughter-in-law Ruth, who came back with her from the region of Moab. (Now they arrived in Bethlehem at the beginning of the barley harvest.)

2. Approximately how long would you say it had been since the people in the village last saw Naomi (Ruth 1:1–4, found on p. 3)?

_____

_____

_____

_____

• *Call me "Mara"* (1:20). That is, "call me 'bitter.'" Naomi tells the townspeople not to call her the name that means "pleasant," but to change her name to "mara," or "bitter." "Mara" has the same root as "myrrh."

• *Treated me harshly* (1:20). The verb here is a different form of the same word "mara." In other words, "Call me Mara for I've been very mara-ed." It appears in a passive form meaning Naomi is the object of someone else's harsh/bitter action. And that someone else is the Almighty, "El Shaddai." Naomi is saying she has been dealt with in such a way that her life has become bitter. "Bitter" does not seem to carry the nuance of "grudge" but of "harsh difficulty," much as we would describe a "bitter winter." Job uses the same form of the word in speaking of how God has dealt with him (Job 27:2). And Habakkuk describes the actions of the Chaldeans by using the noun form of this word (Hab. 1:6).

• *The Sovereign One.* The name for God Naomi uses here is not "Yahweh" or "Elohim," but "El Shaddai." "El Shaddai" is the God who can both bless and judge, the one who gives and takes away, the one in control. Naomi recognizes that the events that have happened to her have fallen within the power of the one who is sovereign.

Naomi is "real" about God. She acknowledges sovereign control, but she also doesn't like what has happened to her, nor does she have to. A former pastor taught us to say this phrase in the midst of difficulty: "I don't like it; I certainly don't understand it, but I trust Him."

What difficult circumstances are you and/or those you love facing?

_____

_____

_____

_____

Do you trust that God is sovereign? What do you think that means?

_____

_____

_____

_____

Does it upset you that El Shaddai could have changed your circumstances but didn't? Why or why not?

_____

_____

_____

A popular book about bad things happening to good people teaches that God is all-loving, but some events fall outside of sovereign control. How do you think Naomi would answer that assessment?

_____

_____

_____

_____

What problem must we wrestle with if we believe events such as tsunamis and horrible diseases and gang rapes and airplanes crashing into World Trade Centers and threats of dirty bombs all fall within God's control?

_____

_____

_____

_____

Do you ever get angry with God? Why or why not?

_____

_____

_____

Do you sometimes feel like you have to explain God's actions? Why or why not?

_____

_____

_____

How honest do you think a Christian can appropriately be in prayer?

_____

_____

_____

• *I left here full, but the LORD has caused me to return empty-handed* (1:21). "Full I went out but empty Yahweh brought me back," is Naomi's wording. Note the contrast between full and empty. Naomi would sound like Yoda if we translated her words in the order she placed them, but note the stress she places on her utter misery.

• *Seeing that the Lord has opposed me* (1:21). Naomi turns up the heat. This was not some active "allowing" God did. Here she says he actively "opposed" or "testified against" her. The expression translated here as "opposed" is to "speak against" or "answer against." It was used in legal contexts with the idea of testifying against or witnessing against. One example has the very same construction. The Book of Micah is set up like a court room argument, and God says, "O My people, what have I done to you? And how have I wearied you? Testify against Me" (Micah 6:3). Others come close:

2 Samuel 1:16—So David said to him, "Your blood is on your own head, for your own mouth has testified against you, saying, 'I have killed the LORD's anointed.'"

Isaiah 3:9—The look on their countenance witnesses against them, And they declare their sin as Sodom; They do not hide it. Woe to their soul! For they have brought evil upon themselves.

Isaiah 59:12—For our transgressions are multiplied before You, And our sins testify against us; For our transgressions are with us,

And as for our iniquities, we know them.

• *The Sovereign One has caused me to suffer* (1:21). El Shaddai caused her to "suffer." While "suffer" is often translated "evil," its usage is not limited to the moral quality of wrongdoing or sin. Note other ways the word is used:

Exodus 5:22—Moses asks God why he has brought calamity on his people.

Numbers 11:11—Moses asks God why he has treated His servant so badly.

Joshua 24:20—God will change his mind and bring calamity on them.

1 Kings 17:20—Elijah cries out to God in bewilderment that He has brought disaster on the widow who has given him lodging.

Micah 4:6—God tells the prophet to assemble the people whom he has afflicted.

Thus Naomi is not saying God has been associated with moral evil, so as to be in cahoots with Satan. Nor is she saying the Lord is anything less than holy, righteous, just, and good. She is saying that El Shaddai is the source of or reason for all the horrifying circumstances she has endured. She holds God ultimately responsible for her misfortune.

7. Do you think Naomi is right? Why or why not?

_____

_____

_____

8. Spend some time in prayer asking for help to trust God's heart even when sovereign ways are a mystery and there is so much pain in the world.

Saturday: Outlaw In-Law

For several years at Dallas Seminary, I served as the teaching assistant for one of the school's homiletics professors. He made it a point to stress to students that preachers should avoid humor when speaking in unfamiliar cultures. Apparently, many jokes fail to transfer well, and nothing can kill a mood in a crowd like a joke landing with a flop. The one grand exception, however—the one topic that cracks up audiences from New York to New Delhi to New Guinea—is the mother-in-law joke. Humor about one's in-laws, sometimes referred to as outlaws, is apparently universal. In fact, it's the mainstay of comedy. You've probably heard some of these:

My mother-in-law is banned internationally from playing poker. She keeps all the chips on her shoulder.

My father-in-law was driving when he saw flashing lights in his rearview window. He pulled over and waited for the officer to walk to his window. When the policeman got there, he said, "Your wife fell out of the car five miles back." My father-in-law wiped his brow. "Whew! I thought I'd gone deaf."

If you lined up all the mothers-in-law in the U.S., and if you laid them end to end, you should leave them there.

What do you call fifty mothers-in-law at the bottom of the ocean? A good start.

Ow!

But at least one evoked a smile, no?

Some of my friends have great in-law relationships. One refers to her son's wife as her daughter-in-love. My friend Erin told me, "I'm thankful that 'in-laws' is not a word that makes me cringe. Though I come from a very different background from my husband, his family has always welcomed me with open arms and encouragement. I actually look forward to being with them through the holidays."

A few years back, when I came into a bit of a windfall, I spent the funds taking my daughter to visit my husband's family. Like Erin, I'm blessed with in-laws I love and enjoy being around.

Such has not always been the case with my mother-in-law, however. My relationship with her started out great and was wonderful for a number of years, but a blow-up at a family reunion left us estranged for a number of years. Today, thank God, we have been truly reconciled to the point that she honored me by asking if I'd serve as her matron of honor when, at age seventy-six, after two decades alone, she married a kind and godly ninety-one-year-old man.

During the time when our contact was limited to exchanging cards at Christmas, I reread the Book of Ruth. And what I saw through the eyes of my own circumstances gave me a whole new level of respect for the book's heroine. I had always assumed Ruth wanted to go with Naomi because Naomi was such a great person. Yet during that read-through I noticed something in the text that hinted otherwise. Naomi told the women of the village that God had brought her back empty-handed. Yet, as mentioned earlier, Ruth was standing next to her when Naomi described herself as empty. How do you think that felt to Ruth, who had told her parents goodbye forever for the sake of this woman?

Sometimes grief makes us oblivious to the love of those around us. And in the face of such grief, Ruth serves as a supreme example of loyal love, of sacrificing her own welfare for that of someone who doesn't even appreciate her, at least initially. Ruth even marries an old guy who probably already has a wife or two, because, by marrying within her husband's family, she can guarantee her husband's name will be remembered. And that means the bitter woman she has followed will have a future. (I can tell you right now I would not marry what my former pastor would call a "geezer" solely to guarantee the well-being of my mother-in-law, even though we're now on great terms!) Now that is sacrificial love. Boaz even recognized how remarkable it was (Ruth 3:10).

If we read Ruth's proposal to Boaz as being about romance, we totally miss the point. She is an example of amazingly loyal, self-sacrificing love, precisely because she was not in love.

A little over a year ago, I fell and broke my collar bone in two. I've had two surgeries requiring grafts from the hip to put me back together. And one morning, while I was still in the hospital recovering from the second operation, I got a picture of that kind of love. Here's how I recorded the event a few days later:

Last Friday morning well before dawn, the tinkling sound of vials carried by a dark form roused me from my morphine-induced slumber. He flipped on the switch over the sink, and the glow offered enough light for me to notice two things. First, the man who entered wore a cheerful white smile on a dark face. And second, Gary, my husband, lay exactly as he had been when I fell asleep—curled at my feet on the vinyl "recliner" where he'd camped since my arrival.

I returned the stranger's smile. He scanned my armband for the UPC code bearing my name and birth date, but he asked my name just to be sure.

"Sandra Glahn," I said. I stared at the so-called bed where my husband lay for a second night while the pleasant stranger wrapped a tourniquet around my arm and slid in a needle. I considered the overrated Hollywood brand of good-times love and pointed to my husband. "See that right there? That's love," I said.

Gary's rhythmic breathing changed slightly. Without opening his eyes, he turned over, his back now toward me. Then he eased into his former rhythm.

"Yeah. Turns over and gives you his back," the man said. His tone sounded affirming, but his words seemed to suggest my husband's change in body language signaled disloyalty. Was the man mocking me? Before I could ask what he meant, he clarified: "That's the sleep of security. He doesn't have to face you. He can turn over and give you his back, and you both know he ain't goin' anywhere."

"You a poet?" I asked. He seemed wise for 4 a.m. thinking.

"I try to be." He flashed me another smile, flicked the switch, and disappeared into the night.

If we make Ruth's story about romantic love, if we relegate it to the Hollywood brand, we miss something important about love. Sometimes sacrifice has nothing to do with romantic feelings. It has to do with loving God. With character. With commitment.

Who are the real "outlaws" in your life? What would happen if you loved them like that?

Prayer: *Heavenly Father, thank You for Your loyal love. Thank you that even though I have nothing to offer you in return other than my worship, You meet my every need. Though I am far less grateful than your goodness deserves, You keep tenaciously showing me your deep unfathomable love. Help me to show others in my immediate and extended families, my church, and my community the kind of "hard" love that Ruth showed to Naomi that others might see in my unconditional kindness something of Your character. In the name of Your Son, Jesus Christ, through whose ultimate sacrifice You lovingly provide access to Your throne, Amen.*

For Memorization: Ruth 1:16–17—But Ruth replied, "Stop urging me to abandon you! For wherever you go, I will go. Wherever you live, I will live. Your people will become my people, and your God will become my God. Wherever you die, I will die—and there I will be buried. May the LORD punish me severely if I do not keep my promise! Only death will be able to separate me from you!"

WEEK 3 OF 4

Boaz and the Barley: Ruth 2

Ruth 1:21—"I left here full, but the Lord has caused me to return empty-handed. Why do you call me 'Naomi,' seeing that the Lord has opposed me, and the Sovereign One has caused me to suffer?"

As a new Christian, I read several Bible studies that instructed me to pray using the acrostic ACTS: Adoration, Confession, Thanksgiving, Supplication (requests). "Always start with adoration, no matter how you feel," somebody told me, "because we should thank God for who He is, not what He has done for us."

Then I went to a church that rearranged the ACTS prayer acrostic to spell CATS: Confession; Adoration; Thanksgiving; Supplication. There a member told me, "Confess first because God can't hear you if you regard iniquity in your heart" (based on a rigid interpretation of Ps. 66:18). It didn't occur to me, at the time, that the Lord's Prayer ends rather than begins with confession.

When my husband and I experienced the pregnancy losses I mentioned earlier, I found myself continually drawn to the psalms. New phrases such as "I was a brute beast before You" (Ps. 73:22) filled my prayers. I had been taught never to question God. Yet consider the questions I encountered in David's poetry:

Psalm 13:1–2 How long, O LORD? Will you forget me forever? How long will you hide your face from me? How long must I wrestle with my thoughts And every day have sorrow in my heart? How long will my enemy triumph over me?

Psalm 22:1 My God, my God, why have you forsaken me? Why are you so far from saving me, so far from the words of my groaning?

While echoing these spiritual gripes, I discovered, to my surprise, that the formulas I'd been taught left out the most common form of psalm in the Bible, the lament. A lament (short for lamentation) is a prayer of complaint—of moaning and wailing. And perhaps, if we followed inspired examples of legitimized whining in the Spirit, if we spent more time fussing to God than to professional listeners, we'd write fewer checks for couch time.

Upon her return to Bethlehem, Naomi told the people, "I left here full, but the Lord has caused me to return empty-handed. Why do you call me 'Naomi,' seeing that the Lord has opposed me, and the Sovereign One has caused me to suffer?" (Ruth 1:21).

I find it ironic that Naomi left due to famine, yet she says she left full. Grief can do that to our perspective. As for her view of God's sovereignty, I think Naomi got it almost right. Ultimately, the Lord of life and death had taken her husband and children from her, and was technically the cause of her suffering. But she got it wrong when she said, "The LORD has opposed me." She had the "what" correct—the circumstances were directed by God. Yet she got the "why" all wrong. But so did David. He asked why God had forsaken Him, but the only person God has ever forsaken was His Son on the cross. And that was so we wouldn't have to be! Sometimes, our grief makes it hard to see straight, and the strange thing is, the awesome thing is, God gives us prayers right there in the Hebrew prayer book (Psalms) for expressing our confusion!

Naomi thought God was against her because she couldn't imagine how El Shaddai could have a good plan that allowed her family to be destroyed. In Dr. Larry Crabb's book, *Shattered Dreams*, he tells how God stripped Naomi of happiness to prepare her for joy. In Ruth, chapter 1, we read that Naomi thinks God is against her. Yet in chapter 2,

Naomi immediately sees the hand of God at work in Boaz's kindness. Crabb asks, "Why was Naomi able to see God's hand when He began to move in her life? Many people can't. Why can she? I think it was because she entered her heart so deeply, feeling all its pain, that she eventually stumbled into the core of her heart, where she wanted God. People who find some way to deaden their pain never discover their desire for God in all its fullness…If we deny how badly we hurt, we remain unaware of our desire for God and aware only of lesser desires."

A friend who miscarried told of how she found sleeping difficult. She said she kept thinking about the baby she lost and crying in the dark. I asked what she thought about going on anti-depressants for a while. Her answer? "I'm not against them if there's a chemical need. But in my case…well…sometimes I think it's good for us to have to wrestle with God in the night."

At one time in my life, I prided myself in never having been upset with God. I took that as a sign of my deep spiritual maturity. The arrogance! It was, rather, a sign that I had not been thrust deeply enough into inexplicable agony.

When the anger kicked in, sometime after the second adoption fell through, I read the Bible cover-to-cover looking for how God's people dealt with such feelings. And you know what I found? God seemed to welcome the negative emotions, even rage, when it led to honest conversation with Him. What upset the Lord didn't seem to be anger. It was when people who were ticked at Him complained to everybody else.

That made a lot of sense. Think of the parallels in human relationships. If I have a beef with my husband, he wants me to come to him, painful as the honest interaction may be, and we'll work it out. Calling all my girlfriends and fussing about him to them is not the way to maintain a healthy relationship. The same is true with God.

ACTS and CATS get us started, sure. But they stop short of taking us deeper. Just like there's no easy formula for living life, there's no formula for conversing with God. What's the cry of your heart? Dr. Crabb said, "If we deny how badly we hurt, we remain unaware of our desire for God and aware only of lesser desires." The converse is true, too. That is, if we admit to God just how badly we hurt, our lesser desires lose their hold on us and we grow attuned to just how much we long for the arms of our heavenly Father after all.

1. Pray for insight, and read chapter 2 of the Book of Ruth:

2:1 Now Naomi had a relative on her husband's side of the family named Boaz. He was a wealthy, prominent man from the clan of Elimelech. **2:2** One day Ruth the Moabite said to Naomi, "Let me go to the fields so I can gather grain behind whoever permits me to do so." Naomi replied, "You may go, my daughter." **2:3** So Ruth went and gathered grain in the fields behind the harvesters. Now she just happened to end up in the portion of the field belonging to Boaz, who was from the clan of Elimelech.

2:4 Now at that very moment, Boaz arrived from Bethlehem and greeted the harvesters, "May the LORD be with you!" They replied, "May the LORD bless you!" **2:5** Boaz asked his servant in charge of the harvesters, "To whom does this young woman belong?" **2:6** The servant in charge of the harvesters replied, "She's the young Moabite woman who came back with Naomi from the region of Moab. **2:7** She asked, 'May I follow the harvesters and gather grain among the bundles?' Since she arrived she has been working hard from this morning until now—except for sitting in the resting hut a short time."

2:8 So Boaz said to Ruth, "Listen carefully, my dear! Do not leave to gather grain in another field. You need not go beyond the limits of this field. You may go along beside my female workers. **2:9** Take note of the field where the men are harvesting and follow behind with the female workers. I will tell the men to leave you alone. When you are thirsty, you may go to the water jars and drink some of the water the servants draw."

Barley is a staple food for humans and animals.
It's less fussy about soil than wheat. Before eating barley, one must remove its outer hull. At this stage, the grain still has its nutritious bran and germ. Hulled barley is considered a whole grain and is a popular health food. Barley may be processed into a variety of products, including flour, flakes similar to oatmeal, and grits. In Judges 7:13 we read that Gideon, who lived at approximately the same time as Ruth, had a dream about a loaf of barley bread. Malted barley is a key ingredient in beer and whiskey production. Check out close-up photos of barley by doing a Google image search or going to "barley" at www.wikipedia.com.

2:10 Ruth knelt before him with her forehead to the ground and said to him, "Why are you so kind and so attentive to me, even though I am a foreigner?" **2:11** Boaz replied to her, "I have been given a full report of all that you have done for your mother-in-law following the death of your husband—how you left your father and your mother, as well as your homeland, and came to live among people you did not know previously. **2:12** May the LORD reward your efforts! May your acts of kindness be repaid fully by the LORD God of Israel, from whom you have sought protection!" **2:13** She said, "You really are being kind to me, sir, for you have reassured and encouraged me, your servant, even though I am not one of your servants!"

2:14 Later during the mealtime Boaz said to her, "Come here and have some food! Dip your bread in the vinegar!" So she sat down beside the harvesters. Then he handed her some roasted grain. She ate until she was full and saved the rest. **2:15** When she got up to gather grain, Boaz told his male servants, "Let her gather grain even among the bundles! Don't chase her off! **2:16** Make sure you pull out ears of grain for her and drop them so she can gather them up. Don't tell her not to!" **2:17** So she gathered grain in the field until evening. When she threshed what she had gathered, it came to about thirty pounds of barley!

2:18 She carried it back to town, and her mother-in-law saw how much grain she had gathered. Then Ruth gave her the roasted grain she had saved from mealtime. **2:19** Her mother-in-law asked her, "Where did you gather grain today? Where did you work? May the one who took notice of you be rewarded!" So Ruth told her mother-in-law with whom she had worked. She said, "The name of the man with whom I worked today is Boaz." **2:20** Naomi said to her daughter-in-law, "May he be rewarded by the LORD because he has shown loyalty to the living on behalf of the dead!" Then Naomi said to her, "This man is a close relative of ours; he is our guardian." **2:21** Ruth the Moabite replied, "He even told me, 'You may go along beside my servants until they have finished gathering all my harvest!'" **2:22** Naomi then said to her daughter-in-law Ruth, "It is good, my daughter, that you should go out to work with his female servants. That way you will not be harmed, which could happen in another field." **2:23** So Ruth worked beside Boaz's female servants, gathering grain until the end of the barley harvest as well as the wheat harvest. After that she stayed home with her mother-in-law.

Underline all the references to "Moab" and "foreign."
What seeming coincidences happen in this chapter?

_____

_____

4. What indications do you see of God's hand at work?

_____

_____

_____

TUESDAY: HARD AT WORK

1. Pray for insight, and read Ruth 2:1–7.

> **2:1** Now Naomi had a relative on her husband's side of the family named Boaz. He was a wealthy, prominent man from the clan of Elimelech. **2:2** One day Ruth the Moabite said to Naomi, "Let me go to the fields so I can gather grain behind whoever permits me to do so." Naomi replied, "You may go, my daughter." **2:3** So Ruth went and gathered grain in the fields behind the harvesters. Now she just happened to end up in the portion of the field belonging to Boaz, who was from the clan of Elimelech.
>
> **2:4** Now at that very moment, Boaz arrived from Bethlehem and greeted the harvesters, "May the LORD be with you!" They replied, "May the LORD bless you!" **2:5** Boaz asked his servant in charge of the harvesters, "To whom does this young woman belong?" **2:6** The servant in charge of the harvesters replied, "She's the young Moabite woman who came back with Naomi from the region of Moab. **2:7** She asked, 'May I follow the harvesters and gather grain among the bundles?' Since she arrived she has been working hard from this morning until now—except for sitting in the resting hut a short time."

2. We know the events in the Book of Ruth took place in springtime, because barley was usually harvested in Israel from late March to late

April. The first chapter of Ruth ends with the statement that Naomi and Ruth arrived in Bethlehem at the beginning of the barley harvest. They didn't appear to plan it that way, but they had impeccable timing. One of the subtle messages woven throughout in this book is that God is in control. Can you think of a time when you saw, in retrospect, God's perfect timing?

_____

_____

_____

_____

3. What does the ability to time such events say about God's power?

_____

_____

_____

Let me go to the fields so I can gather (2:2). Ruth makes a polite request using a Hebrew idiom that's equivalent to "please let me." She doesn't have to be told to get out there and work hard. She's eager to do so.

4. Ruth 2:1 tells us that Naomi's late husband had a relative, a well-off relative, named Boaz. Naomi didn't look him up after she arrived back to town. Did she even know about him? Certainly God knew. Verse 3 says Ruth, "just happened to end up in the portion of the field belonging to Boaz, who was from the clan of Elimelech." The narrative here is written from Ruth's point of view. She didn't plan it that way because she didn't even know. Yet her steps were directed. And if that weren't enough, we find in verse 4, "Now at that very moment, Boaz arrived." Once again we see perfect timing. What seeming coincidences have happened in Ruth's life so far?

_____

5. For the first time in the story we see Boaz, a man who will later appear in both of Jesus' genealogies (Matt. 1:5; Luke 3:32). The text says Boaz arrived from Bethlehem, coming out to the field from downtown. We know from Ruth 3:15 that Naomi and Ruth lived in the city and the fields were outside its gates. What are the first words out of Boaz's mouth (2:4)? How do the workers greet Boaz? What do those words, his and theirs, suggest about him?

_____

_____

_____

_____

To whom does this young woman belong? (Ruth 2:5)—It's difficult to imagine a good man asking a question like this in the twenty-first century, isn't it? A woman as someone's property? Yet in the patri-centric culture in which Boaz lived, a woman belonged either to her father, if she was still single, or to her husband, if married. (It has been said that every woman had to have a male "covering." That's not true, however. A widow or a divorced woman required no such male oversight. See Numbers 30:9.)

Virtually all women at the time were married. And in a world in which *coitus interruptus* was about the only contraceptive option, a married woman could expect to have about twelve children, some of whom would die. That meant women were more vulnerable, requiring much more male protection and provision than is true for women today. In addition, an unmarried female was probably fourteen or younger, so it's not difficult to see the need for supervision. Also, women in Ruth's time were more vulnerable to rape and assault than girls today, who live in houses that lock and counties with jails to house criminals.

Boaz's servant answered his question about whom Ruth "belonged to," telling him that the young woman was the one who had returned with Naomi. That would have told Boaz she belonged to no one. As everyone in the town knew, Naomi and her young daughter-in-law were widows.

Just because the Book of Ruth is a book in the Bible, that does not mean the cultural practices were inspired. And we must take care to avoid reading back into previous times our cultural values, which include a "grid" that includes an enormous population of singles. Paul says singleness can be an even more exalted state than marriage if chosen for the glory of God (see 1 Cor. 7), but in ancient times to be a single woman was certainly not a cultural norm. Even as late as the first century AD, people thought of women in only three categories: virgins (teens), married women, and widows. Neither Greek nor Hebrew has separate words for woman and wife because the two were virtually interchangeable. The same word is used for both, and we have to determine from context which way to translate.

[Ruth] *asked, "May I follow the harvesters and gather grain among the bundles?"* (2:7). Boaz's foreman told him what Ruth had basically asked permission to do what Jewish law required Boaz to allow.

Moses' law made provision for the poor, for resident non-Israelites ("foreigners"), for widows, and for orphans, all of whom were economically disadvantaged. Individuals who fell in these categories were allowed to collect grain from the unharvested corners of the fields.

My father grew up in an agricultural setting in Oregon during the Great Depression in the United States. He tells of how he'd snitch raisins to quell his hunger, and he loved church potluck dinners, because they meant lots of food. My family still places a high premium on giving food as gifts. Every Christmas one of my sisters sends Tillamook cheese, smoked salmon, and boysenberry jam. When I was recovering from surgery last month, my dad sent a box of walnuts and filberts he'd shelled himself. For Christmas, sometimes my parents send marionberry jam. When we visit in the summer, they send us home loaded up with frozen wild blueberries. And last time I visited, my father showed me a sack of onions he had "gleaned," with permission, from a nearby farm. Apparently, the automatic harvesting equipment rounds corners, leaving lots of produce, and Dad couldn't stand to see all those onions going to waste. My parents live in a "seniors" community, and Dad has been known to talk retired high-ranking military officers into helping him pick up day-old bread from grocery stores and deliver it to those in need. Living with hunger has a way of giving someone a deep appreciation for abundance and a distain for waste.

They could also go back over areas where reapers had already harvested to pick up missed or fallen produce, a process called "gleaning." Consider these instructions from the Law:

> **Lev. 19:9–10**—"'When you gather in the harvest of your land, you must not completely harvest the corner of your field, and you must not gather up the gleanings of your harvest. You must not pick your vineyard bare, and you must not gather up the fallen grapes of your vineyard. You must leave them for the poor and the foreigner. I am the Lord your God.

Notice this is repeated four chapters later. Apparently God considered it very important:

> **Leviticus 23:22**—"'When you gather in the harvest of your land, you must not completely harvest the corner of your field, and you must not gather up the gleanings of your harvest. You must leave them for the poor and the foreigner. I am the Lord your God.'"

> Whenever you reap your harvest in your field and leave some unraked grain there, you must not return to get it; it should go to the resident foreigner, orphan, and widow so that the Lord your God may bless all the work you do.

5. From the list of those who were to benefit from these practices, into what categories did Ruth and Naomi fall?

_____

_____

_____

_____

6. God's law placed a high premium on caring for the poor and needy. Sometimes, believers today get the idea that the government will handle the poor so all we need to do is focus on getting out the gospel. Or we express concern that if we develop social programs through which to minister, we will be guilty of preaching the "social gospel." Yet either extreme is wrong, whether we meet only physical or only spiritual needs. God never made such a dichotomy. Jesus didn't say, "Man shall not live by bread, but by every word that proceeds from the mouth of God," he said "by bread alone."

One hundred thirty-six verses in the Bible talk about the poor. James, writing in the New Testament, said, "Pure and undefiled religion before God the Father is this: to care for orphans and widows in their misfortune and to keep oneself unstained by the world" (James 1:27). So caring for the vulnerable is a big priority to God and it's essential to the outworking of our faith.

List vulnerable groups that come to mind (e.g., homeless, persecuted Christians, hungry, communities without water).

_____

_____

_____

Consider how you spend money. How do your spending patterns show concern for members of these groups?

_____

_____

_____

For the poor? For foreigners who can't receive the economic benefits of citizenship?

_____

_____

Orphans?

_____

_____

Widows?

_____

_____

What steps can you take for making these groups a priority in your personal giving? Your time? The focus of ministry in your church?

_____

_____

To understand more about the world in which Ruth lived, picture a time that differed from ours in some key ways:

Commerce revolved around agriculture. The entire economy depended on favorable weather conditions for good crops, which had to be harvested by hand within a relatively narrow window.

The nation had no organized welfare system. Individual farmers were called upon to allow the poor to benefit from their bounty.

Men and women were segregated in their work.

First, the grain had to be harvested, either by pulling it up from its roots, or cutting it with a scythe. Once harvested, it was generally bound in sheaves and gathered into barns or threshing-floors. Threshing involved spreading the sheaves on the floor and having livestock tromp on them or having humans beat the stalks with sticks. Once threshed, grain was separated from its lighter inedible parts, and from dirt, by tossing it up against the wind and catching it (winnowing).

She has been working hard (2:7).—Ruth gets out there and hustles, working hard to bring a good yield by doing physically challenging work. The fields had resting huts, probably to allow for taking short breaks in the shade, to take a drink and to stay hydrated. The foreman tells Boaz that Ruth has rested in the hut "a short time." This is no weak, slouchy, take-care-of-me kind of girl.

What's the hardest physical labor you've ever done?

_____

_____

What is your attitude about work?

_____

_____

Does your work, whether directly or indirectly, benefit others? If not, why not?

_____

_____

_____

WEDNESDAY: YOU REAP WHAT YOU SOW

1. Pray for insight, and read Ruth 2:8–13.

> **2:8** So Boaz said to Ruth, "Listen carefully, my dear! Do not leave to gather grain in another field. You need not go beyond the limits of this field. You may go along beside my female workers. **2:9** Take note of the field where the men are harvesting and follow behind with the female workers. I will tell the men to leave you alone. When you are thirsty, you may go to the water jars and drink some of the water the servants draw."
>
> **2:10** Ruth knelt before him with her forehead to the ground and said to him, "Why are you so kind and so attentive to me, even though I am a foreigner?" **2:11** Boaz replied to her, "I have been given a full report of all that you have done for your mother-in-law following the death of your husband—how you left your father and your mother, as well as your homeland, and came to live among people you did not know previously. **2:12** May the LORD reward your efforts! May your acts of kindness be repaid fully by the LORD God of Israel, from whom you have sought protection!" **2:13** She said, "You really are being kind to me, sir, for you have reassured and encouraged me, your servant, even though I am not one of your servants!"

So Ruth and Boaz have their first conversation.

• *My dear* (2:8).—The most famous movie line of all time starts with Rhett saying to Scarlett, "Frankly, my dear…" While the phrase "my dear" can be affectionate between intimates, or between male/female acquaintances, when the phrase is used between a man and woman who are arguing, it can sound patronizing. Boaz's words do not carry a negative connotation, however. He uses phrasing that shows him to have a kind heart. He wants to put Ruth at ease. And basically, he protects her, cares for her, and even allows her into the inner circle. He far exceeds the requirements of Jewish law.

Share a time when someone showed you unexpected kindness.

_____

_____

_____

To whom can you show kindness through your speech? How?

_____

_____

_____

• *Do not leave* (2:8). Boaz tells Ruth to stay and offers her an amazing deal. He elevates her status from poor woman/gleaner to that of a female harvester, except she gets to take home what she harvests! The boss is going to tell the men not to mess with her, and she even gets to drink from the water someone else has to draw without laboring to carry a jug from home or obtaining water from the well herself. She now has the benefits of a worker. This is a very generous move, which is why it evokes a question.

"Why are you so kind and so attentive to me, even though I am a foreigner?"—Ruth bows her forehead to the ground in a position of total humility. She is stunned by the offer. Not only is she not one of Boaz's workers and not laboring for his benefit, she's also a foreigner. Stigmatized. What possible motive could he have, she wonders?

4. What do the harvest laws tell you about God's character and concern for the needy?

_____

_____

_____

_____

5. What do Boaz's actions tell you about his character before he ever mentions God to Ruth?

_____

_____

_____

6. Whom do you know who could benefit from over-the-top kindness from you?

_____

_____

_____

_____

I have been given a full report (2:11). Boaz gives a reason for his great kindness: word has gotten around about what Ruth did for Naomi. Ruth's husband died, thereby ending any obligation she had to Naomi, so Ruth exceeded the requirements of the law, just like he did. According to Boaz, Ruth did three remarkably selfless things: First, she left her father and mother. Remember, they have no phones, email, IMs, text messages, postal service, or even "photographs to remember you by." This tells us Ruth's parents were still alive when she left, and it's a huge loss for her, on top of already losing her husband. Second, Ruth left her homeland, exchanging the familiar for the unfamiliar. So she's in culture shock. Customs differ, mores differ. She doesn't know the terrain. Or who's related to whom. Have you ever spent time in another country, especially in a small, tightly-knit community? Even where your own language is spoken, it can get dicey.

(Across "the pond" trucks are lorries and a pound is money, not weight.) And that's not to mention the fifty-mile hike Ruth had to take to get to the new domicile. Third, she's living among people she doesn't know. She has not one friend besides Naomi and no prospects of any, since Moabites are second-class citizens. What love she shows!

7. Have you ever been a "foreigner"? If so, how did it feel? Did you commit a *faux pas* or two? If so, what? (I've committed some language blunders that made me turn red from my toes up, but they're too risqué to write here!)

_____

_____

_____

May the Lord reward your efforts! May your acts of kindness be repaid fully by the Lord God of Israel. Now it's clear—Boaz believes in the God of Israel, and he believes God is able to reward and repay fully. This part of the story is not just about a man showing kindness to someone in need, good as that is. This is a righteous man seeking to act with justice and mercy because of his faith.

8. Who do you know that has shown remarkable love? What did he or she do that makes you think that? Pray for that person, asking God to reward such acts of *hesed*.

_____

_____

_____

_____

From whom you have sought protection (v. 12). Boaz uses a metaphor here of God as a bird protecting its young. More literally this is "under whose wings you have sought refuge." So Boaz acknowledges that Ruth has sought refuge "under the wings" of the God of Israel. It appears that Boaz knows she has left Chemosh and embraced the LORD, and he is eager to affirm that decision.

9. Have you sought refuge under the wings of the God of Israel? What kind of relationship do you have with the Lord? What would you like your relationship to be?

_____

_____

_____

_____

10. What is your attitude toward people from other nations? People of difference races? Unbelievers? How do your attitudes line up with God's as revealed in the text?

_____

_____

_____

_____

Thursday: An Astonishing Yield

1. Pray for insight, and read Ruth 2:14–17.

> **2:14** Later during the mealtime Boaz said to her, "Come here and have some food! Dip your bread in the vinegar!" So she sat down beside the harvesters. Then he handed her some roasted grain. She ate until she was full and saved the rest. **2:15** When she got up to gather grain, Boaz told his male servants, "Let her gather grain even among the bundles! Don't chase her off! **2:16** Make sure you pull out ears of grain for her and drop them so she can gather them up. Don't tell her not to!" **2:17** So she gathered grain in the field

until evening. When she threshed what she had gathered, it came to about thirty pounds of barley!

2. Make a list of all Boaz has done for Ruth so far (Ruth 2:8–13).

_____

_____

_____

_____

3. As if all this weren't enough, Boaz does much more (2:14–16).

_____

_____

_____

_____

What does he tell her to do?

_____

_____

_____

_____

What does he give her?

_____

_____

_____

What does he tell his servants to let her do?

_____

_____

_____

How does he tell his servants to aid her?

_____

_____

_____

4. What do you think the other workers thought when the big boss told the Moabitess, "Come here and have some food! Dip your bread in the vinegar" and then gave her roasted grain (2:14)?

_____

_____

_____

5. What do you think the workers thought when Boaz told them to drop grain for her to collect?

_____

_____

_____

Thirty pounds of barley (2:17). The underlying Hebrew says there was an ephah of barley after she beat it out. So, imagine how much there was before she processed it! The NET Bible translators have given the equivalent for today's western audiences (thirty pounds). Pounds and kilos, gallons and liters—different cultures have their own systems of weights and measures. Based on research on the ancient world, this equivalency chart helps us know how much Ruth had at the end of the day:

Ephah of barley (dry)
1 bath (wet measure)
1/10 of a homer
5.8 gallons (wet)
½–⅔ bushel (dry)
29-30 pounds
13 kg[1]

6. How do you think Ruth's haul compares to what she expected to bring home?

_____

_____

_____

7. Have you ever been astounded by God's provision? If so, what were the circumstances?

_____

_____

_____

As was true in Ruth's day, to be widowed or fatherless/orphaned or a resident foreigner today is to be extra vulnerable to injustice and to find it more difficult to gain sustenance. For this reason, as I mentioned earlier, our merciful, just Lord places a high premium on caring for those who fall into these three groups. Consider just a sampling of what God says on the subject:

Exodus 22:22 You must not afflict any widow or orphan. If you afflict them in any way and they cry to me, I will surely hear their

1 *HALOT* 43 s.v.

cry, and my anger will burn and I will kill you with the sword, and your wives will be widows and your children will be fatherless.

Deuteronomy 10:17–18 For the Lord your God is God of gods and Lord of lords, the great, mighty, and awesome God who is unbiased and takes no bribe, Who justly treats the orphan and widow, and who loves resident foreigners, giving them food and clothing.

Deuteronomy 27:19 Cursed is the one who perverts justice for the resident foreigner, the orphan, and the widow.

Psalm 146:9 The Lord protects those residing outside their native land; he lifts up the fatherless and the widow, but he opposes the wicked.

Isaiah 1:17 Learn to do what is right! Promote justice! Give the oppressed reason to celebrate! Take up the cause of the orphan! Defend the rights of the widow!

Isaiah 1:23 Your officials are rebels, they associate with thieves. All of them love bribery, and look for payoffs. They do not take up the cause of the orphan, or defend the rights of the widow.

James 1:27 Pure and undefiled religion before God the Father is this: to care for orphans and widows in their misfortune and to keep oneself unstained by the world.

8. What stands out to you from these passages?

_____

_____

_____

_____

9. List all the ways you can think of to help those who fall into these groups—widows, orphans, and resident foreigners. Here are some examples to get you started: inviting international students to your home; providing monthly support for a child in a developing country; adopting a child; providing foster care; running or contributing to a food pantry; visiting shut-ins; caring for a widowed parent or in-law. Pray, really pray, about about what God would have you do.

1. Pray for God to give you insight into the text. Then read Ruth 2:18–23.

> **2:18** She carried it back to town, and her mother-in-law saw how much grain she had gathered. Then Ruth gave her the roasted grain she had saved from mealtime. **2:19** Her mother-in-law asked her, "Where did you gather grain today? Where did you work? May the one who took notice of you be rewarded!" So Ruth told her mother-in-law with whom she had worked. She said, "The name of the man with whom I worked today is Boaz." **2:20** Naomi said to her daughter-in-law, "May he be rewarded by the LORD because he has shown loyalty to the living on behalf of the dead!" Then Naomi said to her, "This man is a close relative of ours; he is our guardian." **2:21** Ruth the Moabite replied, "He even told me, 'You may go along beside my servants until they have finished gathering all my harvest!'" **2:22** Naomi then said to her daughter-in-law Ruth, "It is good, my daughter, that you should go out to work with his female servants. That way you will not be harmed, which could happen in another field." **2:23** So Ruth worked beside Boaz's female servants, gathering grain until the end of the barley harvest as well as the wheat harvest. After that she stayed home with her mother-in-law.

She carried it back to town (2:18). When was the last time you hoisted a ten-pound bag of dog or cat food onto a shopping cart? Take away the cart, triple the weight, and carry it unassisted all the way from a field to town, and you get an idea of how strong Ruth was. Later we'll see that Boaz loads her up with twice that amount. She's no pale wall-flower damsel in distress waiting to be rescued, that's for sure!

2. Why did Ruth keep the leftovers from the meal (2:18)? What does this tell you about her? How consistent is she in thinking of someone other than herself?

_____

_____

_____

_____

3. Why do you imagine Naomi does not go out in the field with her? (You can totally speculate here. The text doesn't say.)

_____

_____

_____

4. What is Naomi's reaction to the amount of grain Ruth brings home (2:19)?

_____

_____

_____

5. How does Naomi respond when she learns Boaz is responsible for Ruth's hefty haul (2:20)?

_____

_____

_____

6. What reason does Naomi give for wanting God to bless Boaz (2:20)?

_____

_____

_____

This man is a close relative of ours; he is our guardian (2:20). Note that Naomi does not connect Boaz's kindness with any "chemistry" between him and Ruth. This is where seeing romance in the story, at least seeing it too soon, could cause us to miss important details that can teach us something about character. Naomi interprets Boaz's actions as the deeds of a righteous man who is showing kindness, not because Ruth has enchanted him, but because it is the right and gracious thing to do: to care well for one's relatives.

7. What hint do you get that being a field worker was dangerous for a woman (2:22)?

_____

_____

_____

8. According to Ruth 2:23, "Ruth worked beside Boaz's female servants, gathering grain until the end of the barley harvest as well as the wheat harvest." To the best of our knowledge, the wheat harvest lasted another month after the barley harvest was over, so Ruth must have worked in Boaz's fields for about eight weeks. If she took home thirty pounds of grain each day and she took off only one day per week, how much grain did Boaz let her take altogether? (This question is for the math-lovers.)

1440

_____

_____

9. What does the amount tell you about Boaz's generosity and Ruth's industry?

_____

_____

Ruth 2:22—"One day Ruth the Moabite said to Naomi, "Let me go to the fields so I can gather grain behind whoever permits me to do so."

Harvest time provided a short-term opportunity for Ruth to pursue a quick means of support for Naomi and for herself. In Ruth's world, a world without pensions, Social Security, or unemployment insurance, if a childless woman lost her husband, she experienced a catastrophic double-loss. She was bereaved of her husband. But she also could not just go out and pursue a career somewhere to feed herself. Most of the economics happened within the context of the household, as is still the case in many cultures today.

Consider the virtuous woman held up as an example in Proverbs 31. She is a prototype of the wealthy woman living close to the time of Ruth. And she stands as an upper-class example of industry operating out of the home. She had children and a husband, yet she had her own income from buying and selling real estate and trading in belts. Isn't it interesting that this well-to-do woman is still contributing to the economics of her household? Why does she do so? Not so she can have a bigger mansion. She's concerned to "extend her hand to the poor" (Prov. 31:20).

A millennium later, when Paul wanted older women to teach the younger to be "workers at home" (Titus 2:5), he was still operating within a culture in which, to our best understanding, more than 85 percent of the industry happened in the home. There was no such thing as a factory worker and a stay-at-home mom. Both husband and wife were usually stay-at-home parents; both raised kids, taught kids, and participated in industry. Women like Priscilla worked alongside their Aquillas making tents. So Paul was not telling women to be "homemakers" (NKJV) in the way we understand the word today.

The Industrial Revolution completely changed work from primarily a home-based endeavor for both men and women to a factory/home dichotomy. People did ironworks or basketweaving or meat curing or whatever at home. The British writer, Dorothy L. Sayers, writing more than sixty years ago, even before second-wave feminism, penned a marvelous piece in which she noted that much of the restlessness of women happened after the more interesting, mind-engaging work was taken from the domicile (international trade, equipment purchase, negotiation) and put in factories. Couples began to see raising kids as women's work (moms parent, dads babysit) rather than as a partnership. On those few occasions when dads took the kids, and the kids drove 'em crazy, it was often reasoned that women had some special inner thing that made it easier for them to deal with the whining and bickering and tedium. Many failed to appreciate the deep intellectual sacrifices their wives were making to raise their kids.

Sometimes at Christian marriage conferences we teach that the ideal is for moms to be at home, but that's only half of the story. The ideal is for both mom and dad to be home with kids. Now, that doesn't mean they're down on the floor playing with kids all day. Rather, they take their children with them as they support the weak, help the suffering, engage in meaningful (and not so meaningful) work, and get the job done.

We sometimes hold up the Ricky-and-Lucy model, or the Ward-and-June-Cleaver model, as the ideal. We teach "if only..." the church today would get back to that ideal of Ricky going to the club while Lucy cleans or Ward going to the office while June vacuums wearing pearls. (The TV producers say she wore them only because she had a long neck, but I digress.) Truth is, the divorce rate skyrocketed when the men took off for the factories and left their wives at home. It was as high, in fact, as it is now, at a time when it was much more difficult to separate. The effect of the Industrial Revolution on the family has been devastating.

Some point to Paul's admonition that "if a man does not provide for his own, he is worse than an unbeliever" as a prooftext for man-as-breadwinner. They take the phrase right out of 1 Timothy 5. It even has six male pronouns in many English translations. It's all about a husband providing. Or is it? Actually, in the Greek it is "someone" and "one's own," not "he/his." And in the context, Paul is speaking of widows and caring for them. Indeed, the passage is actually more focused on women caring for their mothers and mothers-in-law than it is on men. (See 1 Tim 5:16.)

In the United States, more than a quarter of the population is age 65 or older with disabilities. People are living longer with pensions harder to come by. Ruth and Naomi have much to teach a growing number of those needing care and their caregivers, which should include all of us to some degree. Yes, the work is unglamorous. And it requires deep sacrifice. But we do it by God's grace, not begrudging but kindly, because a mark of godly character has always been showing *hesed* to the vulnerable.

Prayer: *Heavenly Father, thank You for the example of Ruth who sacrificed so much for the sake of someone else, while expecting nothing in return. Thank you for Boaz, who went far beyond what you require in showing compassion and generosity. Thank you that through their story we* *catch a glimpse into Your heart for the poor and vulnerable. Thank you that you care for the widows and the fatherless and the foreigner and the poor. Help me to see places in my heart where I fail to reflect your concern. Please give me wisdom to know how best to use my resources to show your loving-kindness to those in need. Help me to be strong and courageous in my faith, looking for ways to show hesed to others. Thank you that in my spiritual need, you made total provision that I might have access to You and be restored to what you created me to be—a worshiper. I do worship you, Lord, and praise you for who You are. You are so good! In the name of Your Son, our Lord, Amen.*

For Memorization: She replied, "I am Ruth, your servant. Marry your servant, for you are a guardian of the family interests." He said, "May you be rewarded by the Lord, my dear! This act of devotion is greater than what you did before. For you have not sought to marry one of the young men, whether rich or poor. Now, my dear, don't worry! I intend to do for you everything you propose, for everyone in the village knows that you are a worthy woman (Ruth 3:9–11).

Week 4 of 4

A Decent Proposal: Ruth 3–4

Ruth 3:11—"For everyone in the village knows that you are a worthy woman."

A bestselling writer tells men that God gave dominion to Adam and his sons after him. Ahem. *Au contraire, mon frere!* That's true, but it's only half of the story.

Write "women rule" or wear it on a t-shirt, and you risk getting labeled a femiNazi and looked at askance. But women do rule. In fact, subduing the earth, managing its fish and animals and plants, is a big part of what woman was created do to. The first purpose we see for woman—we find it in the mind of God, even before we read the story about woman's creation as "helper"—is that God created humans, both man and woman, to rule the earth. That is the ideal. Consider my source:

> "And God said, Let us make man in our image, after our likeness: and let them have dominion over the fish of the sea, and over the fowl of the air, and over the cattle, and over all the earth, and

over every creeping thing that creeps on the earth. So God created man in his own image, in the image of God created he him; male and female created he them" (Genesis 1:26–27).

While we're talking about bestselling authors, here's another one. There's a big idea floating around that God made men to be warriors and women to be rescued. The damsel in distress thing is super romantic. And it is so not biblical.

Read the Book of Judges. Who wields the tent peg that pierces the enemy's, Sisera's, skull? Ms. Jael, that's who, mighty in battle for God. And what about the woman who pushes a millstone over the wall and kills Abimelech (Judges 9:53)? And you know the woman sometimes labeled "P-31"? She is called a woman of "valor." The section about her in Proverbs starts like this: "A noble woman who can find?" (Prov. 31:10). Well, that same word, noble, or worthy, that Boaz uses to describe Ruth (3:11) is used to describe David's mighty men, only when we translate it there it's "valor." Mighty men of valor.

The entire text of Proverbs 31, which idealizes the excellent wife/woman of valor, is stuffed full of military terms, besides "valor." The biblical ideal of woman is that she is strong and courageous. She is not some pale, Elizabethan, dainty feminine waif who needs rescuing. A suntanned, ripped Ruth hoists bags of grain on her shoulders and takes them to feed vulnerable Naomi.

Moving to the New Testament we find men and women called to suit up with the armor of God and fight (see Eph. 6). Women need a cause for which to fight as much as men do. And we have one!

Some might argue that since The Fall things have changed. I would agree. Yet the ideal hasn't. We don't say it's wrong to buy weed killer, even though weeds were part of the fall. And we don't tell our friends taking language classes that they're out of God's will because God confused languages at Babel. Last I checked, we fight the effects of The Fall rather than embracing them.

In the same way, we should embrace rather than fight against women having dominion in partnership with men.

So women rule. And so do men. Together—male and female. I am not at all suggesting women are superior to men. That's heresy, too. We need each other. But both men and women need to know who women were and are meant to be.

Last summer my family stayed in Timberline Lodge at the foot of Oregon's Mt. Hood. The lodge was built in the 1930s. A short film available in the room gave a fascinating history of the place. And I loved a story some of the old builders told. Apparently, when the men got pretty far along in the lodge's construction, they realized something was missing—the influence of women. Up to a point the whole project had pretty much been a boy's club, so they stopped and found skilled women to labor with them. And the end product, everyone later agreed enthusiastically, was much better for men and women having worked together.

My opera gloves are off to those guys. They came a long way, baby.

Humans rule!

MONDAY: EMPTY TO FULL

1. Pray and ask for insight. Then read Ruth 3 and 4:

Ruth 3

3:1 At that time, Naomi, her mother-in-law, said to her, "My daughter, I must find a home for you so you will be secure. **3:2** Now Boaz, with whose female servants you worked, is our close relative. Look, tonight he is winnowing barley at the threshing floor. **3:3** So bathe yourself, rub on some perfumed oil, and get dressed up. Then go down to the threshing floor. But don't let the man know you're there until he finishes his meal. **3:4** When he gets ready to go to sleep, take careful notice of the place where he lies down. Then go, uncover his legs, and lie down beside him. He will tell you what you should do." **3:5** Ruth replied to Naomi, "I will do everything you have told me to do."

3:6 So she went down to the threshing floor and did everything her mother-in-law had instructed her to do. **3:7** When Boaz had finished his meal and was feeling satisfied, he lay down to sleep at the far end of the grain heap. Then Ruth crept up quietly, uncovered his legs, and lay down beside him. **3:8** In the middle of the night he was startled and turned over. Now he saw a woman lying beside him! **3:9** He said, "Who are you?" She replied, "I am Ruth, your servant. Marry your servant, for you are a guardian of the family interests." **3:10** He said, "May you be rewarded by the LORD, my dear! This act of devotion is greater than what you did before. For you have not sought to marry one of the young men, whether rich or poor. **3:11** Now, my dear, don't worry! I intend to do for you everything you propose, for everyone in the village knows that you are a worthy woman. **3:12** Now yes, it is true that I am a guardian, but there is another guardian who is a closer relative than I am. **3:13** Remain here tonight. Then in the morning, if he agrees to marry you, fine, let him do so. But if he does not want to do so, I promise, as surely as the LORD lives, to marry you. Sleep here until morning." **3:14** So she slept beside him until morning. She woke up while it was still dark. Boaz thought, "No one must know that a woman visited the threshing floor." **3:15** Then he said, "Hold out the shawl you are wearing and grip it tightly." As she held it tightly, he measured out about sixty pounds of barley into the shawl and put it on her shoulders. Then he went into town, **3:16** and she returned to her mother-in-law.

When Ruth returned to her mother-in-law, Naomi asked, "How did things turn out for you, my daughter?" Ruth told her about all the man had done for her. **3:17** She said, "He gave me these sixty pounds of barley, for he said to me, 'Do not go to your mother-in-law empty-handed.'" **3:18** Then Naomi said, "Stay put, my daughter, until you know how the matter turns out. For the man will not rest until he has taken care of the matter today."

Ruth 4

4:1 Now Boaz went up to the village gate and sat there. Then along came the guardian whom Boaz had mentioned to Ruth! Boaz said, "Come here and sit down, 'John Doe'!" So he came and sat down. **4:2** Boaz chose ten of the village leaders and said, "Sit down here!" So they sat down. **4:3** Then Boaz said to the guardian, "Naomi, who has returned from the region of Moab, is selling the portion of land that belongs to our relative Elimelech. **4:4** So I am legally informing you: Acquire it before those sitting here and before the leaders of my people! If you want to exercise your right to redeem it, then do so. But if not, then tell me so I will know. For you possess the first option to redeem it; I am next in line after you." He replied, "I will redeem it." **4:5** Then Boaz said, "When you acquire the field from Naomi, you must also acquire Ruth the Moabite, the wife of our deceased relative, in order to preserve his family name by raising up a descendant who will inherit his property." **4:6** The guardian said, "Then I am unable to redeem it, for I would ruin my own inheritance in that case. You may exercise my redemption option, for I am unable to redeem it." **4:7** (Now this used to be the customary way to finalize a transaction involving redemption in Israel: A man would remove his sandal and give it to the other party. This was a legally binding act in Israel.) **4:8** So the guardian said to Boaz, "You may acquire it," and he removed his sandal. **4:9** Then Boaz said to the leaders and all the people, "You are witnesses today that I have acquired from Naomi all that belonged to Elimelech, Kilion, and Mahlon. **4:10** I have also acquired Ruth the Moabite, the wife of Mahlon, as my wife to raise up a descendant who will inherit his property so the name of the deceased might not disappear from among his relatives and from his village. You are witnesses today." **4:11** All the people who were at the gate and the elders replied, "We are witnesses. May the LORD make the woman who is entering your home like Rachel and Leah, both of whom built up the house of Israel! May you prosper in Ephrathah and become famous in Bethlehem. **4:12** May your family become like the family of Perez—whom Tamar bore to Judah—through the descendants the LORD gives you by this young woman."

4:13 So Boaz married Ruth and had sexual relations with her. The LORD enabled her to conceive and she gave birth to a son. **4:14** The village women said to Naomi, "May the LORD be praised because he has not left you without a guardian today! May he become famous in Israel! **4:15** He will encourage you and provide for you when you are old, for your daughter-in-law, who loves you, has given him birth. She is better to you than seven sons!" **4:16** Naomi took the child and placed him on her lap; she became his caregiver. **4:17** The neighbor women named him, saying, "A son has been born to Naomi." They named him Obed. Now he became the father of Jesse—David's father!

4:18 These are the descendants of Perez: Perez was the father of Hezron, **4:19** Hezron was the father of Ram, Ram was the father of Amminadab, **4:20** Amminadab was the father of Nachshon, Nachshon was the father of Salmah, **4:21** Salmon was the father of Boaz, Boaz was the father of Obed, **4:22** Obed was the father of Jesse, and Jesse was the father of David.

2. What stood out to you as you read?

_____

_____

_____

3. What questions did you have?

4. If you've ever been engaged, how did it happen? If not, what's your favorite engagement story?

5. Do you know of a woman who proposed marriage to a man? If so, what were the circumstances?

6. The odds, humanly speaking, of Ruth avoiding hunger, of marrying, of making a new life for herself were much better back in Moab. Yet at great personal risk, she committed herself to Naomi, and to Naomi's people and her God. Ruth stands as a great example of one who walked "by faith, not by sight" (2 Cor. 5:7). What evidence do you have from her story that faith pleases God and that the Lord is the one who "rewards those who seek him" (Heb. 11:6)?

7. What details in the Book of Ruth encourage you to trust God more fully?

_____

_____

8. Spend some time in prayer placing your trust in God and asking for help to do so completely.

_____

_____

_____

TUESDAY: THE BIG PROPOSAL

1. Pray for understanding and a willingness to be changed by interacting with God's Word. Then read Ruth 3:1–11.

> **3:1** At that time, Naomi, her mother-in-law, said to her, "My daughter, I must find a home for you so you will be secure. **3:2** Now Boaz, with whose female servants you worked, is our close relative. Look, tonight he is winnowing barley at the threshing floor. **3:3** So bathe yourself, rub on some perfumed oil, and get dressed up. Then go down to the threshing floor. But don't let the man know you're there until he finishes his meal. **3:4** When he gets ready to go to sleep, take careful notice of the place where he lies down. Then go, uncover his legs, and lie down beside him. He will tell you what you should do." **3:5** Ruth replied to Naomi, "I will do everything you have told me to do."
>
> **3:6** So she went down to the threshing floor and did everything her mother-in-law had instructed her to do. **3:7** When Boaz had finished his meal and was feeling satisfied, he lay down to sleep at the far end of the grain heap. Then Ruth crept up quietly, uncovered his legs, and lay down beside him. **3:8** In the middle of the night he was startled and turned over. Now he saw a woman lying beside him! **3:9** He said, "Who are you?" She replied, "I am Ruth, your servant. Marry your servant, for you are a guardian of the family interests." **3:10** He said, "May you be rewarded by the LORD, my dear! This act of devotion is greater than what you did before. For you have not sought to marry one of the young men, whether rich or poor. **3:11** Now, my dear, don't worry! I intend to do for you

everything you propose, for everyone in the village knows that you are a worthy woman.

I must find a home for you (3:1). The word for "home" can also have the idea of "rest" and "security." That "rest" does not mean a place for Ruth to kick back, but a place of ongoing provision. Chapter 2 ended with the statement that Ruth worked Boaz's fields during the entire barley and wheat harvests, but then she stayed at home with Naomi. So once the daily loads of barley and wheat ceased, Naomi had to think about economics. What would they eat? How would they eat? The result: "I must find a home for you." Naomi used the same word translated here as "home" back when she urged Orpah and Ruth to return from following her: "May the Lord enable each of you to find security in the home of a new husband!" (Ruth 1:9).

2. Describe the security in your life—spiritual, emotional, and physical. Do you know where your next meal will come from? If you were to sell all you had, how long could you feed yourself?

_____

_____

_____

3. Whom does Naomi see as the one who provides security based on Ruth 1:9? In Ruth 3:1? God? A husband? Herself? All three? How do you think that works out in the mind of this woman who believes so strongly in God's sovereignty?

_____

_____

_____

Tonight [he] *is winnowing barley* (3:2). Naomi's words to Ruth have the word "Look!" stuck in front of them. "Look! He is winnowing barley tonight." The "look!" used to be translated "behold!" but that feels a little antiquated these days. We no longer have a good equivalent. The words "Poof" or "Shazzam" don't cut it. "Lo" is way outdated. Some use "Dang!" (in its positive application). That might work. Or perhaps "Hey!" At any rate, it seems to subtly say, "It just so happened...," giving a nod to God's sovereignty. During the winnowing process, the men would often sleep down at the threshing floor, which was outside the city gates. Imagine the attraction to marauders of that much easily-obtained food.

• *So bathe yourself, rub on some perfumed oil, and get dressed up* (3:3). I don't need to spell this out, do I? Now, why would she tell Ruth to make herself as attractive as possible? To get all fixed up?

Water was and is a precious commodity, but particularly in a time when it had to be drawn from a well or dipped from a stream. And heating water required lots of fuel. In a world without water towers and in-home spigots or faucets, it wasn't so easy to hop in the shower. A full bath was a relatively rare event even up until the last century.

• *Get dressed up* (3:3). Naomi is probably referring to Ruth's outer garment, which may have had several parts to it. Later in the chapter,

---

The word goel *is frequently employed in connection with Hebrew law, where it is the technical term applied to a person who, as the nearest relative of another, is placed under certain obligations.*

(1) If because of poverty a Jew had been obliged to sell himself to a wealthy "stranger or sojourner," it became the duty of his relatives to redeem him (Lev. 25:47).

(2) The same duty fell on the nearest kinsman if his brother, being poor, had been forced to sell some of his property (Lev. 25:23; Ruth 4:4).

(3) It also devolved to the nearest relative to marry the childless widow of his brother (Ruth 3:13).

(4) In Numbers 5:5, the law demands restitution be made to the nearest relative, and after him to the priest, if the injured party has died (Lev. 6:1).

(5) The law of blood-revenge made it the sacred duty of the nearest relative to avenge the blood of his murdered kinsman.

The order in which the nearest relative was considered the goel is given in Lev. 25:48: first a brother, then an uncle or an uncle's son, and after them any other near relative. This order was observed in connection with (1) above, but probably also in the other cases except (4).

Adapted from The International Standard Bible Encyclopedia, "Goel."

Boaz tells Ruth to remove her cloak or cape and hold it out so he can fill it with sixty pounds of grain (3:15). It would have taken lots of fabric to make up a piece of clothing large enough to carry such weight. Regardless of what kind of garment it was, Naomi's intent is obvious. She is preparing Ruth to propose marriage to Boaz, and she wants Ruth to put her best foot a mile forward. Naomi is sending Ruth to get a husband, and Ruth is complying so she can obtain a child for Naomi.

• *Go, uncover his legs, and lie down beside him* (3:4). If you were watching TV with the sound muted and you saw a cake covered with candles being carried toward a child surrounded by singing people, you'd know it was a birthday, wouldn't you? If you saw a dressed-up woman with a guy taking her hand and going down on one knee, what would his body language tell you? You'd know he was proposing marriage, right? We all have our customs. Imagine how strange our customs today would seem (a flaming cake?) to people in places that have different customs for birthdays and engagements.

In the custom of her day, Naomi is telling Ruth how to propose marriage to Boaz. The process may be unfamiliar to Ruth, as Naomi gives much specific detail, ending with the confidence that Boaz will tell Ruth what to do next. And clearly, Naomi trusts Boaz as a God-fearer to act honorably when Ruth places herself in such a vulnerable position by his side late at night. (Naomi's trust is well-founded as the first words out of Boaz's mouth in response to the proposal are words of blessing.)

The NET Bible text here says Naomi told Ruth to "uncover his legs." The word "legs" could also be "the place of the feet," which is how many translators have rendered it. Yet as the word is used in Daniel 10:6, it refers to legs or the leg region. It could also be "foot." During this time in history, "foot" was sometimes a euphemism for genitals (in the same way that "sleep together" can mean "not at all sleeping but doing something else" in our culture). That is why some believe Naomi instructed Ruth to take off Boaz's clothes and expose him. Whether the author intends us to understand it as feet, legs, or "foot," the fact is, Ruth's actions say, "Make me your wife," and nothing in the text hints of impropriety.

• *I will do everything you have told me to do* (3:5). The word order Ruth uses shows she has every intention of following Naomi's instructions to the letter. And, in fact, she does (3:6).

• *Now he saw a woman lying beside him!* (3:8). As a fiction writer/storyteller, I love what happens here in the text. We have to smooth it out to keep it from sounding choppy in translation, but here's what it looks like in a more wooden form: "And look—a woman lying at his feet!" The story teller has jumped into Boaz's point of view to heighten the tension. We're supposed to imagine the scene now from a different perspective. We see it not from that of Naomi and Ruth planning, but from Boaz getting the shock of his life. He's worked hard. He's had a good meal. He's stretched out and dozed off to sleep. He's fallen into a deep, contented rest. Then suddenly, Bam! The eyes fly open. A woman! Not "Ruth" from his perspective, but some unidentified female! Can you feel the shock?

• *I am Ruth, your servant. Marry your servant* (3:9). This translation gives us the intent rather than the euphemism Ruth uses. She says, "Spread your wing (or skirt) over your servant."

Remember in the last chapter where Boaz said Ruth sought refuge under the wing of the God of Israel (2:12)? Ruth tells Boaz here to spread his wing, which is indeed another image for marriage. The word for the corner of a garment was also the word for wing. Ruth is calling attention to what she and Naomi believe are Boaz's legal responsibilities as a kinsman-redeemer. (See sidebar inset.)

Years later this same "garment/wing" image is used regarding marriage in Ezekiel 16:8. God's great *hesed* for the nation is likened to that of a groom for his bride. The Lord says, "'Then I passed by you and watched you, noticing that you had reached the age for love. I spread my cloak over you and covered your nakedness. I swore a solemn oath to you and entered into a marriage covenant with you,' declares the sovereign Lord, 'and you became mine.'"

• *For you are a guardian of the family interests* (3:9). Or "you are a close relative" or a *goel*. Ruth explains why she is proposing. Not "I love you." Not "We'd make a fine couple." But "You're the one responsible." This guardianship was not the same as the levirate arrangement. The word translated "guardian" or "close relative" is sometimes rendered "kinsman-redeemer."

By the time of Naomi, a guardian, or *goel*, had the responsibility for more than property. He was to also care for the widow of his deceased relative. Note the repeated use of this word or a form of it in the Book of Ruth:

3:9 You are the **guardian** of the family interests.

3:12 Yes, it is true that I am a **guardian**, but there is another **guardian** that is a closer relative than I am.

4:4 If you want to exercise your right to **redeem** it, then do so.

4:6 I am not able to **redeem** it, for I would ruin my own inheritance.

4:14 May the LORD be praised, for he has not left you without a **guardian** today!

• *This act of devotion is greater than what you did before* (3:10). There it is again—that word "devotion" or *hesed*. If Ruth impresses Boaz before by her original act of *hesed*—her leaving her parents and homeland to care for Naomi—she blows him away when she proposes to him. He knows she has done so because she wants Naomi to name their future child for her deceased husband, Elimelech, making it possible for his land to be passed down. Boaz is an old guy who probably already has a family. He is certainly not expecting this! What makes Ruth's actions so remarkable to him? "For you have not sought to marry one of the young men, whether rich or poor." Ruth didn't look out for her own interest. She looked out for the interest of someone else to the point that she would marry an old guy like Boaz to guarantee a future for the family of the deceased.

• *I intend to do for you everything you propose* (3:11). Six verses earlier (3:5) we saw the same construction: "All that you say, I will do." There Ruth resolved to do what Naomi proposed. Now Boaz assures Ruth that he's determined to do all she has asked.

• *Everyone in the village knows that you are a worthy woman* (3:11). Boaz gives the reason he will make sure someone, whether the guy who's obligated to do so or he himself, marries Ruth: Because everyone "in the gate" knows she is a worthy woman. "In the gate" could be the entire town, or it could refer to its prominent members, who transacted business at the gate. Either way, the word on the street was that Ruth was a hayil woman.

That word, translated "worthy," (*hayil* is pronounced with a really hard "h" as hi-ILL), is the same word rendered "excellent" or "noble" to describe the ideal wife in Proverbs 31. As mentioned earlier, in other contexts this word is used to describe prowess, bravery, strength, might, or valor in battle. And this word is also translated "noble," as in the case of the noble wife who is a crown to her husband (Proverbs 12:4). Boaz sees Ruth is the poster child for ideal womanhood. What's particularly interesting is that the same word was used to describe Boaz in Ruth 2:1: "[Boaz] was a wealthy, "prominent" (*hayil*) man from the clan of Elimelech."

4. What is it about Ruth that makes Boaz consider her "worthy"?

_____

_____

_____

5. Based on this encounter, what would you say are Boaz's priorities in assessing worth in a woman?

_____

_____

_____

6. Why do you think Ruth's story is included in Scripture? Why did you give the answer you did?

_____

_____

_____

7. What lessons have you learned so far from Ruth's story—what examples to follow and/or values to cherish?

_____

_____

_____

8. List all of the positive qualities you see in Ruth.

_____

_____

_____

_____

9. Spend time praying, asking God to make you a God-trusting, self-sacrificing, hard-working, others-considering, worthy person.

_____

_____

_____

WEDNESDAY: THE PLOT THICKENS

1. Pray for insight. Then read Ruth 3:12–18:

> **3:12** Now yes, it is true that I am a guardian, but there is another guardian who is a closer relative than I am. **3:13** Remain here tonight. Then in the morning, if he agrees to marry you, fine, let him do so. But if he does not want to do so, I promise, as surely as the LORD lives, to marry you. Sleep here until morning." **3:14** So she slept beside him until morning. She woke up while it was still dark. Boaz thought, "No one must know that a woman visited the threshing floor." **3:15** Then he said, "Hold out the shawl you are wearing and grip it tightly." As she held it tightly, he measured out about sixty pounds of barley into the shawl and put it on her shoulders. Then he went into town, **3:16** and she returned to her mother-in-law.
>
> When Ruth returned to her mother-in-law, Naomi asked, "How did things turn out for you, my daughter?" Ruth told her about all the man had done for her. **3:17** She said, "He gave me these sixty pounds of barley, for he said to me, 'Do not go to your mother-in-law empty-handed.'" **3:18** Then Naomi said, "Stay put, my daughter, until you know how the matter turns out. For the man will not rest until he has taken care of the matter today."

- *There is another guardian who is a closer relative than I am* (3:12). What? Where did he come from? Where's he been all this time?

At this point in the story, everybody's heart sinks. The girl who is familiar with this kind man is prepared to marry him. Boaz has said he'd certainly be happy to wed this young woman of worth. And Naomi is ready to see herself joined to the family of such a righteous man. Yet the closer relative has "first dibs." How must Boaz's words about a "closer relative" have sounded to Ruth? Who knows what that nearer relative is like!

- *If he agrees to marry you, fine* (3:13). Property comes with the deal, and the first right of property goes to the closer relative. Boaz determines to follow the law, but assures Ruth he won't make her wait around for him to check into it.

- *I promise, as surely as the Lord lives, to marry you* (3:13). Boaz gives Ruth the best guarantee he can. One way or another she will have a "redeemer." He is happy to oblige and promises with an oath.

- *No one must know that a woman visited the threshing floor* (3:14). Boaz is concerned for "how it might look" that a woman has been at the threshing floor.

2. What might people think if they saw Ruth leaving in the pre-dawn haze? Whose reputation(s) is at stake here?

_____

_____

_____

- *He measured out about sixty pounds of barley into the shawl* (3:15). Once again, Boaz proves himself to be over-the-top generous and Ruth demonstrates she is no wimp. Have you carried sixty pounds from a field into town anytime lately? This provision is Boaz's way of making good on his word. He's providing ample evidence to Naomi that Ruth has been to the threshing floor and has been received favorably.

- *Do not go to your mother-in-law empty-handed* (3:17). Ruth recounts Boaz's words to Naomi. Do you see the beauty in this? Boaz wouldn't let Ruth return "empty handed" to the woman who claimed God brought her back "empty."

3. Did God really bring Naomi back empty? Explain your answer.

_____

_____

_____

Stay put (3:18). Ruth returns to Naomi, who is eager to hear the news. Naomi's instruction to Ruth to "stay put" is probably not so much an imperative to stay inside as to have patience. No doubt Ruth wonders what in the world she has committed herself to. Naomi assures her that Boaz will act quickly. Ruth won't have to wait too long to find out.

4. If someone were to ask Ruth and Boaz what makes a marriage good, what do you think they'd say? Why?

_____

_____

_____

5. English poet and nobleman, Richard Lovelace, at the end of "To Lucasta. Going to the Warres" (i.e., to war) wrote the famous lines, "I could not love thee, Dear, so much/ Loved I not Honour more." Author Calvin Miller said, "Promises and integrity are more important than romance." Do you agree? Why or why not?

_____

_____

_____

6. On a scale of 1–10, rank how much importance you think God places on romantic feelings compared with *hesed*? Why?

_____

7. In a 2005 Valentine's Day op-ed for the *New York Times,* a history professor wrote, "Until 200 years ago, courtship was not typically conducted at dinners by candlelight or trysts under the moon, but negotiated by parents, cousins, neighbors and lawyers in the light of day. People married to consummate a property transaction or political alliance, or to work a farm together. A wedding was not the happy ending to a passionate romance. It was often the unhappy ending to one partner's romance with someone else."[1]

The idea of having full choice about whom we marry is a relatively new concept. Yet arranged marriages wouldn't sit so well with most people today. We were raised on the values of independence, autonomy, and "Make your own way in the world." We tend to assess the health of our marriages by how much "intensity" couples have between them. "Choice" is a key value here. I frankly prefer having some choice in the matter. Still, our neighbors, Christians whose marriage was arranged, say you can grow to love just about anyone who is kind. What are some mixed-up messages our cultures, both the culture at large and the Christian subculture, send about romantic love?

8. If you're married, pray for your own marriage. If single, pray for the marriages of those around you, that they might be filled with sacrificial love.

---

1 Stephanie Coontz, " Historically Incorrect Canoodling" *New York Times*, February 14, 2005.

9. Have you ever had to wait for someone else to determine your future? What was it like? How did it turn out?

_____

_____

_____

_____

10. For what are you waiting right now?

_____

_____

_____

_____

11. If you're in a waiting period, pray and ask God to help you wait well and to trust Him with the outcome.

_____

_____

_____

_____

12. The kinsman-redeemer is a kind of savior who "buys back" what was lost. It has been said that Jesus Christ' is the believer's kinsman-redeemer. In what way is the role of kinsman-redeemer similar to Jesus' work on the cross?

_____

_____

1. Pray for insight. Then read Ruth 4:1–12:

> **4:1** Now Boaz went up to the village gate and sat there. Then along came the guardian whom Boaz had mentioned to Ruth! Boaz said, "Come here and sit down, 'John Doe'!" So he came and sat down. **4:2** Boaz chose ten of the village leaders and said, "Sit down here!" So they sat down. **4:3** Then Boaz said to the guardian, "Naomi, who has returned from the region of Moab, is selling the portion of land that belongs to our relative Elimelech. **4:4** So I am legally informing you: Acquire it before those sitting here and before the leaders of my people! If you want to exercise your right to redeem it, then do so. But if not, then tell me so I will know. For you possess the first option to redeem it; I am next in line after you." He replied, "I will redeem it." **4:5** Then Boaz said, "When you acquire the field from Naomi, you must also acquire Ruth the Moabite, the wife of our deceased relative, in order to preserve his family name by raising up a descendant who will inherit his property." **4:6** The guardian said, "Then I am unable to redeem it, for I would ruin my own inheritance in that case. You may exercise my redemption option, for I am unable to redeem it." **4:7** (Now this used to be the customary way to finalize a transaction involving redemption in Israel: A man would remove his sandal and give it to the other party. This was a legally binding act in Israel.) **4:8** So the guardian said to Boaz, "You may acquire it," and he removed his sandal. **4:9** Then Boaz said to the leaders and all the people, "You are witnesses today that I have acquired from Naomi all that belonged to Elimelech, Kilion, and Mahlon. **4:10** I have also acquired Ruth the Moabite, the wife of Mahlon, as my wife to raise up a descendant who will inherit his property so the name of the deceased might not disappear from among his relatives and from his village. You are witnesses today." **4:11** All the people who were at the gate and the elders replied, "We are witnesses. May the LORD make the woman who is entering your home like Rachel and Leah, both of whom built up the house of Israel! May you prosper in Ephrathah and become famous in Bethlehem. **4:12** May your family become like the family of Perez—whom Tamar bore to

Judah—through the descendants the LORD gives you by this young woman."

Now Boaz went up to the village gate and sat there (4:1). In a world with abundant paper and computer files, we can easily make copies and retrieve records. We have fully staffed courthouses for the keeping of public records. In a world without such resources, however, witnesses and evidence were essential. Such deals required storage in human memories and tangible exchanges that sealed the deal. Lest there be some misunderstanding, numerous witnesses added to the validity of a claim. So Boaz headed for the part of town where people, usually the upper class men, transacted business: the village gate.

We get a similar picture of this sort of setup in Proverbs 31, where the noble-woman's husband, "...is known in the gates, when he sits among the elders of the land" (Prov. 31:23). Only a few walled cities with gates exist today, but at that time, living in a fortified city was a necessity for security. Proverbs 25:28, presumably written by Ruth's great, great grandson, Solomon, says, "Like a city that is broken into and without walls is a man who has no control over his spirit." The entire Book of Nehemiah, written several hundred years later, is about rebuilding the walls of Jerusalem after enemies have knocked them down and carried her people to captivity.

Every night, the city's gates were closed and guards kept watch from atop the walls to assure enemy armies didn't sneak up and attack. Every morning, the gates were opened so travelers could come in and transact business, and insiders could go out to their fields. Everyone going in and out had to pass through the gates, so the elders sat and conducted business transactions in the place with the most traffic.

2. Boaz kept his word to Ruth. No doubt she and Naomi were "sitting on pins and needles" awaiting word of their futures. But Boaz didn't keep them waiting. He followed through immediately. How good are you about quelling others' anxieties when it's in your power to do so? To whom have you made promises you need to keep?

_____

_____

_____

Then along came the guardian whom Boaz had mentioned to Ruth! (4:1). Or "Look! The guardian passed by of whom Boaz had spoken." Once again we have a little word at the beginning that says, "Hey" or "It just so happened that..." The NET Bible translator captures its intent with an exclamation point. We find a subtle suggestion here that something remarkable has happened, as if God were orchestrating events, which, of course, is precisely the case.

3. Once again we see God's sovereign hand working in and through events and timing. In what areas do you need to trust the Lord for His perfect timing?

- *Boaz said, "Come here and sit down, John Doe!' "* (4:1).—Or "Turn aside. Sit here, Mr. So-and-so." In the Book of Ruth, we find name after name. In fact, the author subtly emphasizes that a good name is a significant part of leaving a legacy. The book even ends with a list of names, though a genealogy is not normally included in the "Top 10 Ways to Land a Book." In the midst of this name-filled story, though, one person stands out as nameless: the guy who refused to be Ruth's "kinsman-redeemer." Later we'll see that his reason for shunning his responsibility was out of concern for harming his own inheritance. Boaz, who has sought out this man to seal the transaction says, "Turn aside here *ploni almoni,"* which is a little Hebrew idiom-rhyme for "Mr. So-and-so" or "John Doe." *Ploni Almoni* is the only character in the entire book who remains nameless, which suggests he's the one person we're supposed to forget. He's not worth remembering. How ironic that the guy who sought primarily to secure his own inheritance lost out on a much bigger "inheritance."

- *Boaz chose ten of the village leaders and said, "Sit down here!" So they sat down* (4:2). The village leaders were Boaz's witnesses. He gathered ten witnesses to make the deal official. The text doesn't spell out why Boaz chose that number, and a search of the law reveals nothing that explains the need for so many. Centuries later ten became the number necessary for a Jewish marriage benediction, or a quorum for a synagogue meeting, so Boaz's action here may have set the precedent.

• *Naomi ... is selling* (4:3). Women weren't usually allowed to buy or sell property, but they did have some property rights. Naomi was probably selling the rights. However, rather than what we think of as permanently selling, what she sought to do was more like what we term "leasing." She retained the rights to the property until her remarriage or death. Sometimes people read the Bible and think God has a low view of women because women had so few rights, but the Law actually moved the existing culture closer to God's ideal. It didn't state the ideal; it moved things in that direction. And the culture itself was not inspired!

4. What do you think it would have been like to live in Naomi's day? Do you ever read these stories and come away feeling like God likes men better than women? Why or why not?

• *So I am legally informing you ... you possess the first option to redeem it* (4:4). Boaz deftly lays a trap for the would-be redeemer. How? By leaving out the little detail about the Moabitess.

• *I'll redeem it* (4:4). No question about it. If it's a financial deal, this man wants it. He can afford it.

• *You must also acquire Ruth the Moabite, the wife of our deceased relative, in order to preserve his family name by raising up a descendant who will inherit his property* (4:5). "Uh, by the way, I need to add a footnote," Boaz tells him. "One little detail about this deal..."

Can you feel the man's "uh-oh"? Can you see him squirm? Possibly "acquiring" Ruth along with the land is not an obligation of the Law, but Boaz puts this relative in a position in which he has to act not just according to the minimum requirement, but honorably. All the witnesses add to the pressure. Who's going to be a total selfish heel in front of all the town leaders?

- *The guardian said, "Then I am unable to redeem it"* (4:6). Since Boaz is willing both to lay out the cash and to marry Ruth, and the nearer relative is himself unwilling to do that much, he backs out and tells Boaz the deal's all his. Why?

- *For I would ruin my own inheritance in that case* (4:6). How it would do so is unclear. Perhaps it would take part of an inheritance from the man's other children. We often assume that God would never allow polygamy, but that's reading our times into theirs. While we know from the New Testament that the ideal purpose of marriage is a one-flesh unity that pictures the oneness of Christ and the church, they had no such understanding. Polygamy was far from ideal, but it beat allowing women to starve. Such was God's great heart for the poor and vulnerable. They could not engage in multiple marriages to build their own empires, but adding a near relative to the family, to carry on the name of a relative who died childless, was apparently a righteous thing to do. And this man is more concerned about his own inheritance than caring for his poor relatives.

5. What risks are you willing to take to show *hesed*? Note that the "redeemer" was being asked to show *hesed* to someone he didn't even know. How much are you willing to risk and sacrifice to show God's compassion to the vulnerable?

_____

_____

_____

_____

- *Now this used to be the customary way to finalize a transaction involving redemption in Israel: A man would remove his sandal and give it to the other party. This was a legally binding act in Israel* (4:7). Again, they had no contracts to sign. But the sandal exchange provided tangible evidence that the man had agreed to the terms. It's not all that different from a bride and groom exchanging rings "as a token of our pledge." Why a sandal? It's unclear, but perhaps it symbolically communicated, "Boaz has the right to walk on the land."

• *I have also acquired Ruth the Moabite, the wife of Mahlon, as my wife to raise up a descendant who will inherit his property so the name of the deceased might not disappear from among his relatives and from his village* (4:10). Notice Boaz's reason for marrying Ruth. It's not "because I love this young thing" or "because she's beautiful" or "because she's a hard worker." It's not even "because she's a woman of worth." His reason is completely selfless: to give Mahlon a lasting name. Boaz is now the one showing *hesed*. He's in a position to show grace to the vulnerable—in this case, to Ruth, but ultimately, to Mahlon, her late husband.

• *May the* LORD *make the woman who is entering your home like Rachel and Leah, both of whom built up the house of Israel!* (4:11). As you may recall from the story of Jacob's wives, Rachel and Leah (Gen. 29–30), these two sisters (and their handmaidens) had thirteen children between them—one girl and twelve boys. And those sons became the clan leaders of the twelve tribes of Israel. Sometimes we read the story about how these sisters one-upped each other to compete for the most kids, and we miss that God used even their ruthless competition to accomplish sovereign purposes. That is how their own people remember them—as great founding mothers. Like Rachel, Ruth had been unable to conceive, but God "opened her womb." (In the lives of the Old Testament patriarchs and their wives, infertility often adds to the suspense of how God is going to pull off the impossible to keep his promise to Abraham.)

6. Even Rachel's and Leah's sin didn't thwart God's purposes. In fact, the Lord used all of their one-upping to accomplish great, eternal purposes. That doesn't make their actions right. But it does say a lot about who God is! Think of women who have had abortions who turn around and volunteer at pregnancy resource centers, helping those who face similar decisions. What wrongs have you done that you can offer to God to be used for good?

_____

_____

_____

_____

• *May you prosper in Ephrathah and become famous in Bethlehem* (4:11). The word translated "prosper" is that word for "noble" or "excellent" or "valor" or "strength"—*hayil*, which we discussed earlier. It's the same word used of Boaz (2:1) and Ruth (3:11).

"Ephrathah" and "Bethlehem" are virtually interchangeable. So the people have communicated basically parallel ideas: prosperity is connected with fame, with having renown. The purpose behind God's blessing, as they see it, is to give Boaz prosperity beyond what he already has, which includes a well-known name. In their world, a good name was one's credit rating, one's reputation, one's legacy.

• *May your family become like the family of Perez—whom Tamar bore to Judah—through the descendants the LORD gives you by this young woman* (4:12). If Rachel and Leah aren't strange enough names in a blessing (though strange only at first glance), the people go on to bless Boaz by likening his family to that of Judah and Tamar's! Yet Tamar's is actually a fitting story to bring up in the context of this blessing. Both Ruth and Tamar are extreme examples of loyal love, of going to great lengths to fulfill the law. And both end up in the genealogy of King David, who would have been the focus of this story's original audience.

Incidentally, sometimes we look at Jesus' genealogy and marvel that God used "sinners" such as Tamar, Rahab, and Bathsheba. Perhaps we should marvel even more that God included sinners like Judah! When Judah's father, Jacob, blessed him, he prophesied, "The scepter will not depart from Judah, nor the ruler's staff from between his feet until he comes to whom it belongs and the obedience of the nations is his" (Gen. 49:10). And later Micah prophesied, "As for you, Bethlehem Ephrathah, seemingly insignificant among the clans of Judah—from you a king will emerge who will rule over Israel on my behalf, one whose origins are in the distant past" (Micah 5:2).

7. As you've gone through this study, what commitments have you made to show extreme love? Has the Lord prompted you about someone you need to love well, even though it's difficult? How can you show *hesed*?

_____

_____

_____

_____

_____

8. God isn't finished showing *hesed*! Sometimes we get the idea that if we've blown it, we'll get put on a shelf somewhere. Yet the Lord would much rather redeem our sin, as was the case with Judah. Are you willing to receive God's grace, redemption, and restoration?

_____

_____

_____

_____

9. We can never offer too many thanks to God. What evidence do you have of *hesed* shown to you in the past week? List some examples and offer prayers of appreciation.

_____

_____

_____

FRIDAY: THE STORY IN A LIST

1. Pray for the Spirit to illumine your understanding. Then read Ruth 4:13–22:

> **4:13** So Boaz married Ruth and had sexual relations with her. The LORD enabled her to conceive and she gave birth to a son. **4:14** The village women said to Naomi, "May the LORD be praised because he has not left you without a guardian today! May he

become famous in Israel! **4:15** He will encourage you and provide for you when you are old, for your daughter-in-law, who loves you, has given him birth. She is better to you than seven sons!" **4:16** Naomi took the child and placed him on her lap; she became his caregiver. **4:17** The neighbor women named him, saying, "A son has been born to Naomi." They named him Obed. Now he became the father of Jesse—David's father!

4:18 These are the descendants of Perez: Perez was the father of Hezron, **4:19** Hezron was the father of Ram, Ram was the father of Amminadab, **4:20** Amminadab was the father of Nachshon, Nachshon was the father of Salmah, **4:21** Salmon was the father of Boaz, Boaz was the father of Obed, **4:22** Obed was the father of Jesse, and Jesse was the father of David.

• *So Boaz married Ruth and had sexual relations with her* (4:13). The King James text says Boaz "went into her." Sometimes we expect our Bibles to be G-rated, and they certainly aren't, are they?

• *And the* LORD *enabled her to conceive and she gave birth to a son* (4:13). Or "the Lord gave Ruth conception, and she bore a son." Conception—all life, in fact—is ultimately from the Lord. That doesn't mean people lack faith today if they seek the help of a doctor. Healing from illness is from the Lord, too, but we still consult with gynecologists and oncologists. But the Lord was ultimately the one who gave the infertile woman a new life with a new husband and a baby. And there was no human sacrifice to Chemosh in this culture! Ruth is the ancestress of one Who would be the ultimate human sacrifice, although she dies and centuries pass before anyone realizes just how significant this birth was.

• *And the village women said to Naomi, "May the* LORD *be praised"* (4:14). The woman, remembering *Mara-Noami* saying she has returned "empty" now praise Yahweh because of this grand, sweeping reversal of events.

• *He has not left you without a guardian today* (4:14). The covenant-keeping God has not left Naomi without a "redeemer." This is the only place in the Hebrew Bible where a baby is referred to as a redeemer. Later one will be born in Bethlehem who will epitomize the Baby-Redeemer.

2. Have you ever witnessed an astonishing turn of circumstances? What happened?

_____

_____

_____

_____

3. Do you need God to accomplish a turn-around like this in your life? If so, what are the circumstances?

_____

_____

_____

_____

May he become famous in Israel! (4:14). The "he" to whom the women refer is probably not the Lord, nor Boaz, but Ruth and Boaz's child. The people say, "May his name be famous…" The idiom as it's used here probably means "May his name be proclaimed in Israel" or "…renowned in Israel." "Israel" refers to all of God's covenant people, not just those here in Bethlehem.

4. In Ephesians we read that God is able to do far beyond what we ask or think (3:20). Would you say God made Ruth's child famous in Israel? Beyond Israel? What does this tell you about God?

_____

_____

_____

_____

He will encourage you and provide for you when you are old, for your daughter-in-law, who loves you, has given him birth. She is better to you than seven sons! (4:15). "May he be to you a restorer of life and a sustainer of your old (or hoary) age, for your daughter-in-law who loves you—who is better to you than seven sons—has borne him."

5. Who is the one who ultimately cares for the old and vulnerable according to Ruth 4:15?

_____

Another righteous man in scripture had seven (the perfect number)sons: Job (3:2). He was also well-known and prosperous. Having many sons in previous generations was especially important because sons served as police force, nursing home, grocery store, 401(k) plan, bank, and justice system. So the people here are making a remarkable statement—that this Moabite girl is better than all that. One of her is better than seven of them (4:15)!

6. What do the people say the son will do for Naomi (4:15)?

_____

_____

_____

_____

• *Naomi took the child and placed him on her lap; she became his caregiver* (4:16). This could be translated "...placed him on her breast and she became his nurse." I've heard it said that if a woman wants to provide milk badly enough, she can, and even that Naomi did! My theologian/obstetrician friend, Bill Cutrer, M.D., clarifies: "A 'wet nurse' of course is someone producing milk, and classically is someone who has also given birth recently and continues to produce milk to feed her own and another, or just keeps going after her own is weaned and feeds another. Sometimes an adoptive mom is able to obtain a milk supply by nipple stimulation and a touch of prolactin. Not everyone who tries to do so can, and many need supplementation. Few have such success that they can provide all the milk an infant needs, but some do. For Naomi, Ruth's mother-in-law, to have nursed would have been a miracle at her age and in the technology of the day—to 'wet nurse' twenty-five or more years after giving birth, at age forty or older. A dry nurse was one who cared for the baby, and even fed it, but didn't actually lactate."

Though God is certainly capable of working such a miracle in Naomi, it appears that a dry nurse is what the author had in mind. Naomi, who had her family taken from her, now has a "son" or "descendant." In fact, that is what the people say:

• *The neighbor women named him, saying, "A son has been born to Naomi."* They named him Obed (4:17). It has been said that naming someone in the Old Testament demonstrated the namer's authority, such as the man (*ish*) in the garden calling his wife woman (*ishsha*). Yet, to "call" someone something was usually to give him or her a name that discerned something. In the case of the man, the woman (*ishsha*) was like him (*ish*). In the case of Ruth's neighbor women who name the baby "Obed," his name means "one who serves." That's what sons were for—serving. Obed is seen as the one who will care for Naomi in her "hoary" age. (It may seem unusual that someone other than the parents would name the child, but the underlying Hebrew in this text makes clear that the third-person feminine "neighbor women" were the ones who named Obed.)

• *Now he became the father of Jesse—David's father!* (4:17). The redeemer baby went on to become the grandfather of David, the greatest earthly king ever to rule on the throne of Israel.

Imagine yourself in the audience the first time the genealogy is read. The last word—David—hits like "Pow!" What an ending!

From Ruth 4:18 through verse 22, we get a list of who fathered whom, with Boaz listed seventh and David, tenth:

Perez—Tamar's firstborn
Hezron
Ram
Amminadab
Nachshon
Salmah/Salmon
Boaz—The righteous man in our story
Obed—The baby redeemer
Jesse
David—(Jesse's youngest) The great king

In democracies, genealogies are usually far less important than in monarchies, where they are essential. At the time this genealogy was written, such lists established position, authority, and power in various political and societal contexts. They also served to teach. Genealogies were sometimes "edited" down to include only five and ten generations. The list started with the patriarchs, the founders, the clan fathers. And it ended with the well-known recent generations. The middle is where names of the lesser-known were dropped out.[2]

7. What are some things we can conclude about God's sovereign hand as we look at this list?

_____

_____

_____

_____

8. Think of the circumstances surrounding your own birth and family circumstances. For what—good and bad—do you need to trust the *hesed* and sovereignty of God? Give thanks for who God has made you and for the circumstances that have made you what you are.

_____

_____

_____

_____

9. In Ruth we see several benedictions or blessings pronounced. People in Ruth's time took such blessings much more seriously than we do when we say "Happy New Year" or "Happy Birthday." Their benedictions were said in the form of a prayer, with the expectation that God would accomplish them:

[2] K. Lawson Younger, Jr. *The NIV Application Commentary: Judges/Ruth.* (Grand Rapids, Michigan: Zondervan), 2002, p. 404.

Naomi to Ruth and Orpah (Ruth 1:9)—"May the Lord enable each of you to find security in the home of a new husband!" Then she kissed them goodbye and they wept loudly.

Boaz to Ruth (Ruth 2:12)—"May the Lord reward your efforts! May your acts of kindness be repaid fully by the Lord God of Israel, from whom you have sought protection!"

The people of the town and the elders to Boaz (Ruth 4:12)—"May your family become like the family of Perez—whom Tamar bore to Judah—through the descendants the Lord gives you by this young woman."

A. How does the verse below demonstrate that God has brought these blessings to pass?

_____

_____

_____

_____

_____

Ruth 4:18—These are the descendants of Perez: Perez was the father of Hezron...

B. What does it suggest about God's ability to answer prayer?

_____

_____

_____

_____

_____

10. Now that you've considered the entire story in the Book of Ruth, what do you see as its main messages?

_____

_____

_____

Perhaps your list looks something like this:

• God kept his promise to preserve his covenant people.

• God is in control.

• God's purposes are good.

• God cares for the needy including the poor, the widow, and the resident foreigner.

• God richly rewards those who show *hesed* to the vulnerable.

• God answers prayer.

• God is able to bless beyond what we will ever know in ways we cannot imagine.

11. From what you've studied, list specific ways in which you have seen God's character and nature demonstrated:

_____

_____

_____

12. Have you taken refuge under the wings of the Lord? Have you trusted in the one who redeemed us as "foreigners" in a strange land? Do you worship and glorify the Sovereign One? Do you have faith in the one who rewards seekers? If so, express it through prayer. If not, why not? What questions remain?

_____

_____

_____

_____

From a story about two widows, we gain beautiful insight into how God uses shattered dreams to release us to better futures and more fulfilling lives. We, who have Ruth's and Naomi's whole story, know better than they did, don't we? We can see the big picture of how it all turned out.

The first time I saw the movie, "Jurassic Park," I watched the more intense scenes through salty buttered fingers. I kept covering my face, worried that the dinosaurs would eat the kids, yet too curious to take my eyes off the screen. Finally, my husband, who had already seen the film, leaned over and whispered, "The kids won't die." Once I knew that, I could put my hands back in my lap and relax. Knowing the ending, I could endure the terror that preceded it.

Perhaps you stand in the middle of your own story. Maybe you feel like God opposes you because your circumstances hurt so much it's hard to read them any other way. The apostle Paul, writing a thousand years after Ruth, said that all creation writhes in pain like a woman in natural childbirth awaiting its ultimate redemption (Rom. 8:22). So let's be honest, as Naomi was, about our pain. The ending is happy, but the stress before the end is real.

Still, like my husband who knew the kids in Jurassic Park wouldn't die (hope I didn't ruin the ending for you!), we know how this story ends: Another baby born in baby-Obed's town took away the penalty for our sin. And some day He will mount David's throne to reign on earth as king. And the calf will lie with the lion (Isa. 11:6). The Lion from Judah's Tribe will overcome (Rev. 5:5). Every knee from Irian Jaya to India to Iraq to Afghanistan to Asia to Africa to South America to Australia to the United States of America will bow and every tongue confess that He is Lord to the glory of God the Father (Phil. 2:10). As Julian of Norwich said in the fifteenth century, "All shall be well and all shall be well and all manner of thing shall be well."

"Thy kingdom come!"

SATURDAY: I DREAM OF—GENEALOGY?

Ruth 4:14–15 "The village women said to Naomi, 'May the Lord be praised because he has not left you without a guardian today! May he become famous in Israel! He will encourage you and provide for you when you are old, for your daughter-in-law, who loves you, has given him birth. She is better to you than seven sons!'"

I love to write suspense fiction. It's the closest to creating *ex nihilo*

I'll ever get. Out of nothing—poof. I dream and worlds appear.

It's fun to make up characters. Maybe my protagonist should have purple highlights, drive a Karmann Ghia, and attend the University of Oregon. Or maybe I'll make her gray-haired, smoking a stogie, and walking with a limp. Should I write into being an evil green-eyed guy who wears his shirts starched, has a penchant for Deusenbergs, and plays the mandolin? Or should I make him a snowboarder?

And the food! I can whip up grilled pork roast, guilt-free alfredo sauce, and crème brûlée in a puff pastry. And the setting? The Sahara. Antarctica. Or a planet of my own making, complete with a talking chimera in a canteena.

Whatever I do, one thing is certain: I have to create a plot that holds readers captive so they neglect the laundry, the bathtub, sleeping, breathing. The last thing I'll do, if I want to tell a dramatic story, is include a long list of names in my story's climax. That would be like rolling the credits as the main action of a movie rather than as the P.S.

About a quarter-century ago, *Reader's Digest* published a special edition of the Bible, billed as a condensed edition. Fifty-five percent of the Old Testament and 25 percent of the New Testament got cut in the effort to make the Bible "accessible" to those who never, or rarely, read it. Among the first texts pulled? The "begats."

Yet leave it to God to break all the rules when breathing inspiration into the best-told stories of all time. Ending with a genealogy is exactly what He has the human author do in the Book of Ruth. And once we "get" what He's doing, we have to admit He has provided an utterly dramatic landing.

The readers of "Ruth" lived in a world before moving pictures. No videos. No photos. Only drawings. So when a loved one died, the bereaved had no hope of ever seeing so much as a likeness of that person's face again. Ever. The only thing left was a memory, and a name, and hopefully a child, preferably a son, to carry these on. If you loved someone, you wanted to make sure his or her name was never forgotten. To the descendants of Abraham, genealogy ruled.

The writer of Matthew, addressing a Jewish audience, begins his Gospel about Jesus' life by tracing the Lord's royal pedigree. Ruth's name in Matthew's genealogy is the only place her name appears in the New Testament. Yet, considering it's the genealogy of our Lord, it's not a bad place, is it?

In the list of names at the end of the Book of Ruth, we have the ancient version of the family photo album. And what might seem anticlimactic to us, thrilled the readers of Ruth's story. Why? The last name on that list was King David.

What Ruth could not have known, but those who heard her story would have quickly picked up on, is that God continued to bless her long after her death. She went on to be the grandmother of the greatest earthly king ever to live. And it just keeps getting better by the time we get to Matthew. The last name in Matthew's genealogy list is the Lord Jesus Christ!

Back when I was in seminary, my Hebrew professor and the Old Testament department chair, Dr. Bob Chisholm, observed, "Ruth concludes with a genealogy which seems anticlimactic for the narrative to end. However, closer inspection shows how it fits the context. By tracing Perez through Boaz and on to David, the narrator shows that the prayers of blessing offered earlier in the chapter were fulfilled. God made Boaz famous and gave him an unbroken line of male descendants, culminating in David. This reminds us God does bless the faithful, even after their lifetime and more than they can imagine."

A Moabite girl, a young gentile, a female born outside the nation of Israel and having the wrong pedigree in every way is grafted into the royal tree. And her progeny include the greatest earthly king ever to live, and the ultimate King who will reign forever and ever. All this happened because she embraced Yahweh as her God and showed astonishingly loyal love to a grieving, initially-ungrateful mother-in-law.

When Ruth's son was born, the people in her community prayed God would bless her lineage. Those who read the Book of Ruth know the Self-Existing One did exactly that. So they see that God answers prayers—beyond imagination—offered by the obedient who show loyal love even after they are long gone. That's just the kind of God our Lord is. And El Shaddai, is still looking to pour out His blessing on faithful followers today.

Prayer: *O Great I AM, O Sovereign One, You who keep Your word to a thousand generations, You who love mercy and justice and humility, who care for the needy and the vulnerable, I worship you! Thank You that You are in control. Help me to trust Your perfect ways and Your perfect timing, because You are able and You are good. Thank you that you care for the poor, the widow, the resident foreigner, the desperate. Thank you that You reward those who care for "the least of these." Help me be attuned to their cries that I might be more like You. Thank you that even though you are so great as to control every part of the universe, You bend your ear to hear my every prayer. Who am I that I should be the object of such great love? Thank you that you are able to do far beyond what I can even ask or imagine. Glorify Yourself through my life that I might shine forth something of Your glory to a desperately hurting world. I ask these things in the name of my Redeemer and King, Jesus Christ, the Son of David, the Son of God. Amen.*

For Memorization: Ruth 4:11–12 "All the people who were at the gate and the elders replied, 'We are witnesses. May the LORD make the woman who is entering your home like Rachel and Leah, both of whom built up the house of Israel! Then you will accomplish great things in Ephrathah and be famous in Bethlehem. May your family, the descendants the LORD gives you through this young woman, be like the family of Perez, whom Tamar bore to Judah!'"

CLOSING THOUGHTS

In the dark era of the judges in Israel's history, the story of Ruth, like spangled stars across a black sky, glimmers with God's faithfulness and love. While the Israelites were off doing what "everybody thought was right in their own eyes" (Judges 21:25), a poor, childless widow from a pagan land exemplified how those who truly follow Yahweh live. She left the familiar comfort of her parents, her friends, and her community to settle in enemy territory, where she certainly faced ostracizing glares. There she cared for her poor, vulnerable, grieving mother-in-law. And through the life of this penniless woman we see how a God, who is rich in mercy, provided a great leader, King David, for the nation called out to be an entire kingdom of priests (Exod. 19:6).

All of the events in the Book of Ruth were orchestrated, they "just so happened," through a set of impossible, pathetic circumstances and a faithful God-fearing woman. And the birth of Ruth's grandson mentioned at the end of the book, foreshadows the rise of an even greater King—one whose kingdom will have no end.

We tend to think of kings as ruling and having authority. Yet in the days prior to the period of judges, God gave some specific instructions to Moses about what an Israelite king was to do, in addition to giving orders, when he rose to the throne. Moses recorded these instructions in what we now know as the Book of Deuteronomy:

> "When you come to the land the LORD your God is giving you
> and take it over and live in it and then say, "I will select a king like

all the nations surrounding me," you must select without fail a king whom the LORD your God chooses... When he sits on his royal throne he must make a copy of this law on a scroll given to him by the Levitical priests. It must be with him constantly and he must read it as long as he lives, so that he may learn to revere the LORD his God and observe all the words of this law and these statutes and carry them out. Then he will not exalt himself above his fellow citizens or turn from the commandments to the right or left, and he and his descendants will enjoy many years ruling over his kingdom in Israel" (Deut 17:14, 18–20).

One of my mentors suggested that I purchase a lined journal and do as the king did—write out the entire Book of Deuteronomy. It was no small task, as it took about a year of Sundays in one- or two-hour segments. But I finally finished! The beauty of the assignment was that it forced me, in this urbanized, crowded, noisy, hectic, techno-interrupted world, to slow down and think about every syllable in the text. I was astounded by the holiness of God, as I paid close attention to the blessings and cursings promised to Israel, depending on whether they obeyed. I noticed details I'd glossed over in earlier readings, too. Odd names stuck out. Repeated locations took on complex histories as I connected what God did in a town, and then returned to do another work, and another, in the same place.

In college, when I studied Paul's epistles, my professor assigned a similar project. Each time we studied a book, whether it was Galatians or even the über-long Book of Acts, he had us write out the book in longhand. We outlined with charts, so we got the big idea, and then filled them in with every word from the text. And we used colored pencils to highlight repeated words. We meditated on the thoughts as we carefully crafted them, and we grew to appreciate how easy it was for a scribe to miss a word or an entire line, especially when two lines started with the same letter, or worse, the same word.

Now it's your turn. In the space provided, spend the next few days writing out the Book of Ruth. (It's only eighty-five verses. Deuteronomy has thirty-nine *chapters*!)

As you write, chew on the storyteller's words. Notice the sovereign hand of God at work. Think about what a high premium the Lord places on caring for the needy. Marvel, as you write out the genealogy, how God weaves a story through human lives. Don't rush to complete the assignment. Take your time and notice details. Ask questions.

Such slow interaction with God's word is more than an antidote to protect us from the poison of our fast times. It's a form of meditation, which comes with the rewards promised in Psalm 1. The person who meditates on God's word, the psalmist tells us, is like a tree firmly planted by rivers of water, which brings forth fruit in its season.

So pray for insight and begin. Enjoy!

The Book of Ruth

Ruth 1

1:1 During the time of the judges there was a famine in the land of Judah. So a man from Bethlehem in Judah went to live as a resident foreigner in the region of Moab, along with his wife and two sons. **1:2** (Now the man's name was Elimelech, his wife was Naomi, and his two sons were Mahlon and Kilion. They were of the clan of Ephrath from Bethlehem in Judah.) They entered the region of Moab and settled there. **1:3** Sometime later Naomi's husband Elimelech died, so she and her two sons were left alone. **1:4** So her sons married Moabite women. (One was named Orpah and the other Ruth.) And they continued to live there about ten years. **1:5** Then Naomi's two sons, Mahlon and Kilion, also died. So the woman was left all alone—bereaved of her two children as well as her husband! **1:6** So she decided to return home from the region of Moab, accompanied by her daughters-in-law, because while she was living in Moab she had heard that the LORD had shown concern for his people, reversing the famine by providing abundant crops.

1:7 Now as she and her two daughters-in-law began to leave the place where she had been living to return to the land of Judah, **1:8** Naomi said to her two daughters-in-law, "Listen to me! Each of you should return to your mother's home! May the LORD show you the same kind of devotion that you have shown to your deceased husbands and to me! **1:9** May the LORD enable each of you to find security in the home of a new husband!" Then she kissed them goodbye and they wept loudly. **1:10** But they said to her, "No! We will return with you to your people."

1:11 But Naomi replied, "Go back home, my daughters! There is no reason for you to return to Judah with me! I am no longer capable of giving birth to sons who might become your husbands! **1:12** Go back home, my daughters! For I am too old to get married again. Even if I thought that there was hope that I could get married tonight and conceive sons, **1:13** surely you would not want to wait until they were old enough to marry! Surely you would not remain unmarried all that time! No, my daughters, you must not return with me. For my intense suffering is too much for you to bear. For the LORD is afflicting me!"

1:14 Again they wept loudly. Then Orpah kissed her mother-in-law goodbye, but Ruth clung tightly to her. **1:15** So Naomi said, "Look, your sister-in-law is returning to her people and to her god. Follow your sister-in-law back home!" **1:16** But Ruth replied,

"Stop urging me to abandon you!

For wherever you go, I will go.

Wherever you live, I will live.

Your people will become my people,

and your God will become my God.

1:17 Wherever you die, I will die—and there I will be buried.

May the LORD punish me severely if I do not keep my promise!

Only death will be able to separate me from you!"

1:18 When Naomi realized that Ruth was determined to go with her, she stopped trying to dissuade her. **1:19** So the two of them journeyed together until they arrived in Bethlehem.

When they entered Bethlehem, the whole village was excited about their arrival. The women of the village said, "Can this be Naomi?" **1:20** But she replied to them, "Don't call me 'Naomi'! Call me 'Mara' because the Sovereign One has treated me very harshly. **1:21** I left here full, but the LORD has caused me to return empty-handed. Why do you call me 'Naomi', seeing that the LORD has opposed me, and the Sovereign One has caused me to suffer?" **1:22** So Naomi returned, accompanied by her Moabite daughter-in-law Ruth, who came back with her from the region of Moab. (Now they arrived in Bethlehem at the beginning of the barley harvest.)

Ruth 2

2:1 Now Naomi had a relative on her husband's side of the family named Boaz. He was a wealthy, prominent man from the clan of Elimelech. **2:2** One day Ruth the Moabite said to Naomi, "Let me go to the fields so I can gather grain behind whoever permits me to do so." Naomi replied, "You may go, my daughter." **2:3** So Ruth went and gathered grain in the fields behind the harvesters. Now she just happened to end up in the portion of the field belonging to Boaz, who was from the clan of Elimelech.

2:4 Now at that very moment, Boaz arrived from Bethlehem and greeted the harvesters, "May the LORD be with you!" They replied, "May the LORD bless you!" **2:5** Boaz asked his servant in charge of the harvesters, "To whom does this young woman belong?" **2:6** The servant in charge of the harvesters replied, "She's the young Moabite woman who came back with Naomi from the region of Moab. **2:7** She asked, 'May I follow the harvesters and gather grain among the bundles?' Since she arrived she has been working hard from this morning until now—except for sitting in the resting hut a short time."

2:8 So Boaz said to Ruth, "Listen carefully, my dear! Do not leave to gather grain in another field. You need not go beyond the limits of this field. You may go along beside my female workers. **2:9** Take note of the field where the men are harvesting and follow behind with the female workers. I will tell the men to leave you alone. When you are thirsty, you may go to the water jars and drink some of the water the servants draw."

2:10 Ruth knelt before him with her forehead to the ground and said to him, "Why are you so kind and so attentive to me, even though I am a foreigner?" **2:11** Boaz replied to her, "I have been given a full report of all that you have done for your mother-in-law following the death of your husband—how you left your father and your mother, as well as your homeland, and came to live among people you did not know previously. **2:12** May the LORD reward your efforts! May your acts of kindness be repaid fully by the LORD God of Israel, from whom you have sought protection!" **2:13** She said, "You really are being kind to me, sir, for you have reassured and encouraged me, your servant, even though I am not one of your servants!"

2:14 Later during the mealtime Boaz said to her, "Come here and have some food! Dip your bread in the vinegar!" So she sat down beside the harvesters. Then he handed her some roasted grain. She ate until she was full and saved the rest. **2:15** When she got up to gather grain, Boaz told his male servants, "Let her gather grain even among the bundles! Don't chase her off! **2:16** Make sure you pull out ears of grain for her and drop them so she can gather them up. Don't tell her not to!" **2:17** So she gathered grain in the field until evening. When she threshed what she had gathered, it came to about thirty pounds of barley!

2:18 She carried it back to town, and her mother-in-law saw how much grain she had gathered. Then Ruth gave her the roasted grain she had saved from mealtime. **2:19** Her mother-in-law asked her, "Where did you gather grain today? Where did you work? May the one who took notice of you be rewarded!" So Ruth told her mother-in-law with whom she had worked. She said, "The name of the man with whom I worked today is Boaz." **2:20** Naomi said to her daughter-in-law, "May he be rewarded by the LORD because he has shown loyalty to the living on behalf of the dead!" Then Naomi said to her, "This man is a close relative of ours; he is our guardian." **2:21** Ruth the Moabite replied, "He even told me, 'You may go along beside my servants until they have finished gathering all my harvest!'" **2:22** Naomi then said to her daughter-in-law Ruth, "It is good, my daughter, that you should go out to work with his female servants. That way you will not be harmed, which could happen in another field." **2:23** So Ruth worked beside Boaz's female servants, gathering grain until the end of the barley harvest as well as the wheat harvest. After that she stayed home with her mother-in-law.

Ruth 3

3:1 At that time, Naomi, her mother-in-law, said to her, "My daughter, I must find a home for you so you will be secure. **3:2** Now Boaz, with whose female servants you worked, is our close relative. Look, tonight he is winnowing barley at the threshing floor. **3:3** So bathe yourself, rub on some perfumed oil, and get dressed up. Then go down to the threshing floor. But don't let the man know you're there until he finishes his meal. **3:4** When he gets ready to go to sleep, take careful notice of the place where he lies down. Then go, uncover his legs, and lie down beside him. He will tell you what you should do." **3:5** Ruth replied to Naomi, "I will do everything you have told me to do."

3:6 So she went down to the threshing floor and did everything her mother-in-law had instructed her to do. **3:7** When Boaz had finished his meal and was feeling satisfied, he lay down to sleep at the far end of the grain heap. Then Ruth crept up quietly, uncovered his legs, and lay down beside him. **3:8** In the middle of the night he was startled and turned over. Now he saw a woman lying beside him! **3:9** He said, "Who are you?" She replied, "I am Ruth, your servant. Marry your servant, for you are a guardian of the family interests." **3:10** He said, "May you be rewarded by the LORD, my dear! This act of devotion is greater than what you did before. For you have not sought to marry one of the young men, whether rich or poor. **3:11** Now, my dear, don't worry! I intend to do for you everything you propose, for everyone in the village knows that you are a worthy woman. **3:12** Now yes, it is true that I am a guardian, but there is another guardian who is a closer relative than I am. **3:13** Remain here tonight. Then in the morning, if he agrees to marry you, fine, let him do so. But if he does not want to do so, I promise, as surely as the LORD lives, to marry you. Sleep here until morning." **3:14** So she slept beside him until morning. She woke up while it was still dark. Boaz thought, "No one must know that a woman visited the threshing floor." **3:15** Then he said, "Hold out the shawl you are wearing and grip it tightly." As she held it tightly, he measured out about sixty pounds of barley into the shawl and put it on her shoulders. Then he went into town, **3:16** and she returned to her mother-in-law.

When Ruth returned to her mother-in-law, Naomi asked, "How did things turn out for you, my daughter?" Ruth told her about all the man had done for her. **3:17** She said, "He gave me these sixty pounds of barley, for he said to me, 'Do not go to your mother-in-law empty-handed.'" **3:18** Then Naomi said, "Stay put, my daughter, until you know how the matter turns out. For the man will not rest until he has taken care of the matter today."

Ruth 4

4:1 Now Boaz went up to the village gate and sat there. Then along came the guardian whom Boaz had mentioned to Ruth! Boaz said, "Come here and sit down, 'John Doe'!" So he came and sat down. **4:2** Boaz chose ten of the village leaders and said, "Sit down here!" So they sat down. **4:3** Then Boaz said to the guardian, "Naomi, who has returned from the region of Moab, is selling the portion of land that belongs to our relative Elimelech. **4:4** So I am legally informing you: Acquire it before those sitting here and before the leaders of my people! If you want to exercise your right to redeem it, then do so. But if not, then tell me so I will know. For you possess the first option to redeem it; I am next in line after you." He replied, "I will redeem it." **4:5** Then Boaz said, "When you acquire the field from Naomi, you must also acquire Ruth the Moabite, the wife of our deceased relative, in order to preserve his family name by raising up a descendant who will inherit his property." **4:6** The guardian said, "Then I am unable to redeem it, for I would ruin my own inheritance in that case. You may exercise my redemption option, for I am unable to redeem it." **4:7** (Now this used to be the customary way to finalize a transaction involving redemption in Israel: A man would remove his sandal and give it to the other party. This was a legally binding act in Israel.) **4:8** So the guardian said to Boaz, "You may acquire it," and he removed his sandal. **4:9** Then Boaz said to the leaders and all the people, "You are witnesses today that I have acquired from Naomi all that belonged to Elimelech, Kilion, and Mahlon. **4:10** I have also acquired Ruth the Moabite, the wife of Mahlon, as my wife to raise up a descendant who will inherit his property so the name of the deceased might not disappear from among his relatives and from his village. You are witnesses today." **4:11** All the people who were at the gate and the elders replied, "We are witnesses. May the LORD make the woman who is entering your home like Rachel and Leah, both of whom built up the house of Israel! May you prosper in Ephrathah and become famous in Bethlehem. **4:12** May your family become like the family of Perez—whom Tamar bore to Judah— through the descendants the LORD gives you by this young woman."

4:13 So Boaz married Ruth and had sexual relations with her. The LORD enabled her to conceive and she gave birth to a son. **4:14** The village women said to Naomi, "May the LORD be praised because he has not left you without a guardian today! May he become famous in Israel! **4:15** He will encourage you and provide for you when you are old, for your daughter-in-law, who loves you, has given him birth. She is better to you than seven sons!" **4:16** Naomi took the child and placed him on her lap; she became his caregiver. **4:17** The neighbor women named him, saying, "A son has been born to Naomi." They named him Obed. Now he became the father of Jesse—David's father!

4:18 These are the descendants of Perez: Perez was the father of Hezron, **4:19** Hezron was the father of Ram, Ram was the father of Amminadab, **4:20** Amminadab was the father of Nachshon, Nachshon was the father of Salmah, **4:21** Salmon was the father of Boaz, Boaz was the father of Obed, **4:22** Obed was the father of Jesse, and Jesse was the father of David.